CW00499077

Falling In Love: A Church With A Small Congregation.

By Robin Pritchard

About the Author

Robin Pritchard was born in County Durham in 1953. In 1984 he was ordained a priest in the Church of England and retired from parish ministry in 2017. As well as being a Priest, he enjoys writing novels. In 2010 he gained an MA in Creative Writing from the Anglia Ruskin University. As well as this book, his second Christian work, he has also written the following novels: *The Urban Mystic, A History of Mermaid, The Plagiarist, That Murderous Tree* and *The I in Me.* He has also published the Christian book *Honey from the Rock.*

If you enjoy this book, would you be kind enough to write a review on Amazon and give me some stars. If you would like to help me to improve my writing in future, please contact me through my author's page. Thank you. Contact: wotlwots@btinternet.com

[7] **The law of the LORD is perfect, converting the soul: the testimony of the LORD is sure, making wise the simple.** Psalms 19:7 (KJV).

[6] **The LORD preserves the simple;**
when I was brought low, he saved me. Psalms 116:6 (ESV).

Post communion Collect for Lent 5 - Passion Sunday:

Lord Jesus Christ,

you have taught us

that what we do for the least of our brothers and

sisters

we do also for you:

give us the will to be the servant of others

as you were the servant of all,

and gave up your life and died for us,

but are alive and reign, now and for ever. Amen.

A BEGINNING

[12] ***When they were few in number, very few indeed,*** **and resident aliens in Canaan,** [13] **wandering from nation to nation and from one kingdom to another,** [14] **he allowed no one to oppress them; he rebuked kings on their behalf:** [15] **"Do not touch my anointed ones, or harm my prophets."** Psalm 105:12-15 (CSBBible**).**

I find a gathering of emotion in my mind as I begin this book. Love itself is complicated to define when it is with another human being, but the task of describing one's love for an institution or a community adds a different layer of difficulty. How even to begin? Yet, I believe, God has laid it on my heart not to shirk the task. I have tried very hard not to be critical. I intend it to be an observation. Where I have failed, please forgive me. If I succeed, I hope it will be to give a church with a small congregation its worth. They have their own dignity.

I retired from my parish ministry because my hearing impairment had become so pronounced that I could no longer carry out all my duties. Coping with the secrets of the quiet-voiced at the back of church and leading PCC meetings, by deciding who was speaking, searching around for clues from lips and other people's responses had become impossible. I discovered that I was not retired because I was a 'disabled person', but that – and I now use the PC way of describing myself – it was because I was a person with a hearing disability or impairment. The PC way is to acknowledge that I am no less a person because I lack some specific ableness and that my disability does not define me. My hearing loss is an unfortunate consequence of an incomprehensible something, nobody knows what, that means I must constantly take a rather pragmatic view of how much I can join in the joy of human conversation.

I would like to borrow that language to describe 'small churches'. This is the last time I will use such a phrase in the book as I wish to avoid it. And I only use it now because this is common parlance: big churches and small churches, people say. I would like to suggest right from the outset that they are either churches with small congregations [a CWASC singular & CWASCs plural] or churches with large congregations [a CWALC singular & CWALCs plural]. I agree it will be difficult if I use this acronym throughout, but I would be undermining my own argument if I did not. If I were to pursue that other way of describing them - small - then it quickly leads to those other judgemental things that people add to 'church' to describe a CWASC. My church, during most of my ministry, was a CWASC, and described, along with other such churches, as weak, failing and fragile. In a culture which favours numbers and the ability to pay the Parish Quota it was inevitable that such descriptions grew to be common currency in Deanery Synod meetings, for instance.

I hope you will understand then, when I tell you that this book was born in part out of my outrage that God's precious CWASCs should be so despised. I mean this as an observation and not a criticism.

To use the PC language that places the word church first is to restore the beginnings of a true understanding of what a church is, and, in my opinion, why the CWASC is one of the jewels in God's crown. The size of the congregation becomes irrelevant when we define what a church is. I am no less of a person because I cannot hear; I am no less human, less of who I am in myself as well as who God sees me. In some cases, I am more so, as my disability has taught me so much, and has been used innumerable times as a vehicle by which God has displayed his love for me.

This book then is not a comparison of the virtues of a CWASC over a CWALC or even a criticism of a CWALC. However, you may construe it as a defence of something that I and many others love deeply.

I ask then is a CWASC disabled in any way? Has it got limbs missing? Does it not have the chance to hear God as clearly or speak up for him loudly? Can it not model what it is to live an authentic Christian life?

Right back at the beginning of the church when the apostles are arrested and stand trial, after Gamaliel's defence of them, we read

42 **Every day in the temple, and in various homes, they continued teaching and proclaiming the good news that Jesus is the Messiah.** Acts 5:42 (CSB).

We find no mention of size. And:

21 **At that time he rejoiced in the Holy Spirit and said, "I praise you, Father, Lord of heaven and earth, because you have hidden these things from the wise and intelligent and revealed them to infants. Yes, Father, because this was your good pleasure.** Luke 10:21 (CSB).

This verse continues to build the argument that perhaps the carefully worked out principles of church growth may indeed be better understood by the, so called, maligned, infantilised, failing and weak churches who are the CWASC.

May not a CWASC and its ministry experience an anointing by God like any other church? God's whole treatment of humanity has been kind and overgenerous. Are we not to follow such a pattern in all things?

It is inevitable that as a priest in the Church of England this book will carry a strong flavour of a church that largely expresses itself through parish ministry that focusses on an actual building. It is often the size and quality of these buildings and the contrast with the number who occupy it that creates the dichotomy of CWASC and CWALC and leads to the impressions and judgments that follow. It is these impressions and judgements that I wish to contradict.

N.B. Most Bible quotations are from the CSB and retain their American spelling.

SECTION A – REBUTTING CRITICISM

CHAPTER 1 – Is A CWASC < CWALC?

For if someone comes into your meeting wearing a gold ring and dressed in fine clothes, and a poor person dressed in filthy clothes also comes in, [3] if you look with favor on the one wearing the fine clothes and say, "Sit here in a good place," and yet you say to the poor person, "Stand over there," or "Sit here on the floor by my footstool," [4] have not you made distinctions among yourselves and become judges with evil thoughts? James 2:2-4 (CSB).

Inevitably, this is a treatise against arrogance, against belittling and judging harshly those things that God does not. It should be counterintuitive to disrespect what God does not, but it is so easy to do and oh so satisfying at times. I am the first to admit that my brain, apparently unhinged from my will, goes about this daily work of appraising and condemning the people I come across, based on the scantest evidence, and leads to countless occasions where I must admit to myself that I misjudged a person or a situation. As you can see, I am aware of how easy it is to do! Nevertheless, 'judge not your brother or sister' must also include, 'do not judge your brother's or sister's church, or minister, or style of worship, or theology, or apparent lack of success,' without knowing all the facts.

Is it possible for us to say that a CWASC is as of equal value to a CWALC? Does not the 'church bit' remain constant, regardless of the size of the worshiping community gathered there? We would not call a baby any less a human being because it is dwarfed by an adult, and its size and immaturity are less than a mature adult. Neither can we call the aged person or housebound, with very little mobility or opportunity, any less human. Humanity is not defined or expressed by ability or reach, and neither is the description of a group of people as a church. It is not my purpose in this book to bring you reams of detail on the theology of church, but I am guessing that nowhere in those piles of theological reflection that have been produced does the amount of money a group of people have, or their numerical strength, come into it.

**35 They remembered that God was their rock, the
Most High God, their Redeemer. 36 But they deceived
him with their mouths, they lied to him with their
tongues, 37 their hearts were insincere toward him, and
they were unfaithful to his covenant. 38 Yet he was
compassionate; he atoned for their iniquity and did not destroy them. He often turned his anger aside and did
not unleash all his wrath. 39 He remembered that they
were only flesh, a wind that passes and does not return.**
Psalms 78:35-39 (CSB).

How wonderful this is. God appears to be more compassionate towards our failure, towards our fleshiness, even to being a CWASC, one that is as worthless as critics suggest. God's ability to see potential and redemption in humankind is at the core of his being. He makes allowances for us.

C S Lewis in his book Miracles comments, *'Christ did not die for men[sic] because they were intrinsically worth dying for, but because He is intrinsically love, and therefore loves infinitely. And what, after all, does the size of a world or a creature tell us about its 'importance' or value?...*

The conclusion is inevitable: the importance we attach to greater differences of size is an affair not of reason but of emotion – of that peculiar emotion which superiorities in size begin to produce in us only after a certain point of absolute size is reached.'

How big does a church need to become before it appears on the radar of CHURCH and gets included on the map? What are our criteria for determining its success by its performance? Indeed, how do we intend to measure performance? Have we not gone astray somewhere?

CWASCs are not the enemy of CWALCs such that they can be bypassed, rooted out and destroyed. They are not a waste of the money paid in ministry, or a waste of space. They do not hold back the church unless the church regards itself as an institution that must remain spare and lean – like an army in which only the young and fit are welcome. They do not need to be starved for their own good. Maybe more resources should be paid to the vulnerable than the not so. Consumerism and such allied philosophies have no place in The Church or should it take any part in defining what a church is. What is important is not size but depth of spirituality.

In previous years of education practice there was much talk of Value Added. For example, if a school in an urban priority area managed to improve the educational ability of its pupils significantly from their starting point, as they entered the school, in comparison to when they left, this was Value Added. It counted as a higher achievement even if the end level educationally may be lower than that of other schools. When the assessment criterion were changed, such schools were deemed failing and Ofsted was sent in. It depends on where you start.

Is this principle not also true of a murderer serving a life sentence in prison who comes to Christ and, with his help, begins to deal with his anger issues? Progress may be made but he may still never come up for parole. The decent person who comes to Christ may have no such compulsion to make any progress at all and remains happy to hide behind his inherent goodness and social grace. A CWASC may start at the bottom of the ladder and not make as much progress to raise its leg over any imagined bar of success, but even so it may have attained more in Value Added that many other churches.

2 Ascribe to the LORD the glory due his name; worship the LORD in the splendor of his holiness. Psalms 29:2 (CSB).

CHAPTER 2 – Those Weak, Fragile And Failing Churches.

[3] **I will not set anything worthless before my eyes.** Psalms 101:3 (HCSB).

If a CWASC really is a weak, failing and fragile church, as some describe it pejoratively, then, by definition, it must also be useless, unimportant, insignificant and worthless. What can we learn from these adjectives? And if it really is worthless then, as Psalm 103 tell us, God will have nothing to do with it. And yet countless testimonies show that God is at work in CWASCs. So, either God has decided to go against his own nature, to give such churches a second chance or it is not true to say that they are worthless. I believe that God does not see such churches with the critical, condemning eye that equates their numerical limitation with failure.

[7] **"Do not look at his appearance or his stature... Humans do not see what the Lord sees, for humans see what is visible, but the Lord sees the heart.** 1 Samuel 16:7 (CSB).

God does not judge by appearances. We might see some crumbling edifice in a little village, with a barometer outside that shows how much is still to be raised of the half a million pounds to repair the roof, and think that represents the worshipping heart of the congregation that meets within. God does not. The whole physicality, its appearance, the smell of the dusty interior distracts us from what may be happening there. As might the clothes of a refugee, worn daily over many months of perilous travel: the smelly threadbare clothes of a highly skilled surgeon, fleeing a political regime that pursued him. The heart of a church is not the building. God looks at the heart of the people for whom it is a shelter on a Sunday. They, if you asked them, probably see it as a beautiful and special sort of home, worth repairing if they had the cash, for their spiritual community. Church buildings exist all over our country from the smallest hamlet to the biggest city. They have congregations of different sizes. The secular world sees these buildings as the church, but we dare not allow ourselves to do so. God's x-ray vision looks directly through the walls and focusses specifically on the community in it. He looks at the heart of such a community and the individual hearts of those who make it up. Would we really want to worship a God whose only narcissistic thought was how his glory appeared reflected in the building itself? Would we really want to worship a God whose only narcissistic thought was how his glory is enhanced by the number of worshippers inside it? When Solomon dedicated his temple, the glory of God drove the people from the building. There will be no glory to God unless there is a good heart among the people who worship there:

But the seed in the good ground — these are the ones who, having heard the word with an honest and *good heart*, hold on to it and by enduring, produce fruit. Luke 8:15 (CSB).

And neither does God necessarily choose his followers, those of ***good heart,*** from the successful of the world:

...Not many were wise from a human perspective, not many powerful, not many of noble birth. 27 Instead, God has chosen what is foolish in the world to shame the wise, and God has chosen what is weak in the world

to shame the strong. [28] God has chosen what is insignificant and despised in the world — what is viewed as nothing — to bring to nothing what is viewed as something, [29] so that no one may boast in his presence. 1 Corinthians 1:25-29 (CSB).

And Paul himself recognising the counterintuitive approach of God:

[9] But he said to me, "My grace is sufficient for you, for my power is perfected in weakness." Therefore, I will most gladly boast all the more about my weaknesses, so that Christ's power may reside in me. [10] So I take pleasure in weaknesses, insults, hardships, persecutions, and in difficulties, for the sake of Christ. For when I am weak, then I am strong. 2 Corinthians 12:9-10 (CSB).

Indeed, it seems that God goes for insignificant on purpose:

[7] "The LORD had his heart set on you and chose you, not because you were more numerous than all peoples, for you were the fewest of all peoples. [8] But because the LORD loved you... Deuteronomy 7:7-8 (CSB).

[10] For who despises the day of small things? Zechariah 4:10 (CSB)

God shows no partiality it appears. He can, may and often chooses what the world considers to be small, weak, fragile and failing. Or he can choose a CWALC [a Church with a large congregation] if he so wishes. They are not the opposite ends of a spectrum; they all fall within his loving circle of The Church.

[15] **...Do not be partial to the poor or give preference to the rich; ...I am the Lord.** Leviticus 19:15-16 (CSB).

It appears that God is better qualified to make such judgments than we are:

[34] **For who has known the mind of the Lord? Or who has been his counsellor?** Romans 11:34 (CSB).

We have missed something by ignoring how both weakness and vulnerability give God a special opportunity to work his will in the lives of our churches and ourselves. At the end of the day: **...the Lord's portion is his people,** Deuteronomy 32:9 (CSB).

Wherever they are, or how few can meet, they are his.

It is true that these churches are often mainly older people, but in the immortal words of why we were encouraged to obey the Covid lockdown, 'Do not kill granny.' At the very least older people deserve spiritual care until death and should not be abandoned.

In his book *The Bruised Reed,* the Puritan pastor Richard Sibbes reflects: *'As a mother is tenderest to the ... weakest child, so does Christ most mercifully incline to the weakest. Likewise, he puts an instinct into the weakest things to rely upon something stronger than themselves for support. The vine stays itself upon the elm, and the weakest creatures often have the strongest shelters. The consciousness of the church's weakness makes her willing to lean on her beloved, and to hide herself under his wing.'*

CHAPTER 3 – The Problem With Numbers.

...[Jesus] called the Twelve, Mark 9:35 (CSB); **...the Lord appointed seventy-two others,** Luke 10:1 (CSB); **...Nymphia and the church in her home.** Col 4:15 (CSB); **For where two or three are gathered together in my name, I am there among them.** Matthew 18:20 (CSB).

Do numbers really matter?

What is too small? Is there a point at which falling numbers in a church deny it the title church? Two or seventy-two? Church growth principles have shown that Moses' father-in-law's astute advice, to break the people of Israel into more manageable numbers, had something to say all those years ago:

The next day Moses sat down to judge the people, and they stood around Moses from morning until evening... 17 "What you're doing is not good," Moses's father-in-law said to him. 18 "You will certainly wear out both yourself and these people who are with you, because the task is too heavy for you. You can't do it alone. 21 But you should select from all the people able men, God-fearing, trustworthy, and hating dishonest profit. Place them over the people as commanders of thousands, hundreds, fifties, and tens... 24 Moses listened to his father-in-law and did everything he said. Exodus 18:13-26 (CSB).

From a simple ministerial perspective, from the point of view of the human frailty and energy levels of ministers, there are natural limits to how big a congregation can be without dividing it up. CWALCs usually have more than one minister. It was a popular theory in the early days of Church Growth research that there was a maximum number beyond which churches would not grow, and an upper limit to whom a single minister could relate to. They were advised to split the congregation into house fellowships with their own sub-minister. Does each one become a church for that moment it meets, because it meets in the house belonging to... a modern day Nymphia? And what of a CWASC that only has enough people to fill one house group? When we begin to analyse what we mean by church simply by numbers, the whole exercise becomes ludicrous. Jesus himself, refusing to define an exact number, talks more in terms of whether he is there, present with the people, or not.

Are we complete, a CWASC may ask, or more likely, are we complete enough? They will know only too well that some of the gifts that are mentioned in the Bible, that one would find in a church, are conspicuously absent from their own. Does it matter? They might feel a real sense of bereavement and anxiety, shame even, because once they were a bigger church numerically. It does not need others to suggest you are a failure, the word can haunt you even if nobody articulates it. And when we are bereaved and made anxious by a feeling of failure, we lack confidence and become less effective. Rather than penalise the CWASC and talk them down, we need to talk them up. We need to find ways of bolstering their confidence.

Cannot we say to them, 'Yes, despite your small numbers you are still completely a church.'

Why can we say that? Because they have formed a body of Christ in their place, warmed by the presence of God and full of trust that God has provided all they need, and that any lack he will make up. Surely if Jesus is there, they are complete?

God does not worry about being few. In the instructions for celebrating the Passover from Exodus we read:

[4] **If the household is too small for a whole animal, that person and the neighbor nearest his house are to select one based on the combined number of people; you should apportion the animal according to what each will eat.** Exodus 12:3-4 (CSB).

There is always a way around smallness. I am quite a tall person and, on several occasions over the years, I have had to reach down groceries in a supermarket for someone less blessed with height. If, in addition, the definition 'smallness' becomes wrongly correlated with lacking self-reliance or feebleness, then we will fail to search for the potential strengths that such characteristics bring in God's economy. We will be in trouble and very unbiblical to boot. Jesus tells us not to judge, for if we do, we will incur judgment ourselves. We may judge a CWASC in some way, questioning their right of survival, but in return God will judge our smallness and meanness of spirit.

This is not saying that God will treat every church the same. It is right and appropriate to be aware of the reach of any church and its potential, but God is better at making such judgments than we are. **Increase the**

inheritance for a large tribe and decrease it for a small one. Numbers 26:54 (CSB).

There is a clear example in the trouble David got into by counting the number of troops Israel had. Why did he do it? Was it to put his mind at rest? Perhaps he felt he would then be able to say, 'I have enough troops at my command to defend our nation and for us to live in peace,' quite forgetting that in several of his major battles it was due to the Lord that he won. God loves small numbers and impossible odds: see the story of Gideon, who sent troops home at the instigation of God to make the victory more glorious for him and to bring greater honour to his name.

David was shown his mistake: because of the counting, the strength of Israel was tested by the Lord by a plague that destroyed five percent of the fighting men.

[5] **So the LORD sent a plague on Israel from that morning until the appointed time, and from Dan to Beer-sheba seventy thousand men died.** 2 Samuel 24:15 (CSB).

Perhaps by having a lot of troops he thought to spare God; or worst still, perhaps it was a selfishness that motivated him and he wanted to glory in the power of his realm. He was straying towards a Nebuchneezzarean attitude to what he owned and what he had achieved. God hates human pride because it disavows him from the heart of such a person.

David's conscience troubled him after he had taken a census of the troops. He said to the Lord, "I have sinned greatly in what I have done. Now, Lord, because I have been very foolish, please take away your servant's guilt." 2 Samuel 24:10 (CSB).

Small is good anyway. The book of Proverbs tells us that ants, hyraxes, locusts and lizards buck the usual world reaction to small. Ants are not strong, but they provide adequately for themselves. Hyraxes live in cliffs. Locusts have no king but are a mighty army. A lizard is so vulnerable he can be caught easily, but he lives unmolested in a king's palace. The conclusion though is that they are full of wisdom:

Four things on earth are small, yet they are extremely wise: Proverbs 30:24 (CSB).

This verse begins the song of praise that extols the virtues of these small creatures.

God retains a generosity to those in need beyond anything. His love remains exemplary for the disadvantaged and vulnerable. And this includes churches!

He gives strength to the faint and strengthens the powerless. Isaiah 40:29 (CSB).

In any case we are over reliant on large numbers: at the final judgment we may find ourselves in thin company. Might is not right. Great numbers do not win the day. God's judgments are inscrutable and are nothing to do with rewarding power.

14 **How narrow is the gate and difficult the road that leads to life, and few find it.** Matthew 7:14 (CSB). and **"For many are invited, but few are chosen."** Matthew 22:14 (CSB).

We will never win the numbers game with God. And as if to back it up: **"The Lord had his heart set on you and**

chose you, not because you were more numerous than all peoples, for you were the fewest of all peoples. But because the Lord loved you... Deuteronomy 7:7,8 (CSB).

We may be far wiser to separate ourselves from any large group and find a better home among the few!

Just imagine: the strength of a CWASC, reconciled to its capabilities, frees it from worrying about diminishment and failure.

CHAPTER 4 – The Remnant.

[5] In the same way, then, there is also at the present time a remnant chosen by grace. [6] Now if by grace, then it is not by works; otherwise grace ceases to be grace. Romans 11:5-6 (CSB).

I am of a generation that, when I was a child, used to go to 'real sales' with my mum. Shops nowadays seem to have perpetual sales on. When I was a child we looked forward to the January sales with some anticipation - and quite rightly so, as real bargains could be picked up.

My mother used to take me to Soper's [which became a Debenhams] in Harrow, North London for the sale, where we endured an hour-long queue, or more, in the freezing cold just so mum could be one of the first into the shop. Her speciality subject was the REMNANT sale. My Mum was a great needlewoman and used to go once a year to stock up on material - end of rolls mainly - to keep her going through the year. Have you ever been to a REMNANT sale? An awesome event! Where else would normally temperate women become so aggressive?

This kind of image of the REMNANT is to be found in the Bible and is appropriate for our reflection.

[7] Then the remnant of Jacob will be among many peoples like dew from the LORD, like showers on the grass, which do not wait for anyone or linger for mankind. Micah 5:7 (CSB).

This idea of a Remnant pops up consistently throughout Scripture. It appears at those times when the Hebrews are on their uppers, at the point of being swept away by circumstances; when their state seems hopeless. And it is not simply because their situation is hostile to them, but mainly because God seems against them too and has turned his back on them. Well almost. God is unable to deny his own nature as a God of compassion, who cannot hold his anger for ever, and so saves them. I often find I would make a worse God than he does because I get angry on his behalf with those who have no respect for him and I would not give in so easily and rescue them!

Of course, there were times when he seems to be so incandescent with rage that he appears to genuinely have given up completely, like at the time of The Flood. Then we find, he organised for a Remnant to survive – Noah and his family. He even promised that he would never get that angry again!

So even as God's anger flares and appears to consume all, yet we find among the ashes, protected by him from the fiercest heat, lies a minute residue of the people of faith, those who have not turned away from him: like the seven thousand people of Elijah story; like Lot and his family; Daniel and his friends who will not bow the knee to the prevalent evil of the day. Thus, this Remnant become as special in God's sight as the majority were who rejected and opposed him. On this Remnant he bestows great favours. He is a giving God and he must give to be true to his nature. All that immense love must constantly have a focus outside himself or he might implode, explode or cease to be God. Those born of fire will become in themselves a refreshment for the people.

You will be struggling to fit this image to the one you probably carry in your mind of the CWASC: these poor churches who, on first sight, appear to be on their last gasp. I must add here that I am not blind to the faults and malfunctions of the CWASC and these will be addressed later in the book. However, it would be wrong not to begin with God. Who are we to question God's affection? If he chooses to give a full day's wage to those who labour for only part of the day who are we to gainsay it?

Thus, we can become part of the REMNANT of the church in England as we accept that truth for ourselves and find that God has let us off because he can and because he wants too. How releasing - we are ushered in to a time of pleasing God because we want to and not because we must.

Is it not a drag when somebody expects you to do something for them? You know if you do not do it, they will be disappointed, but if you do then, because they expected it, there is no kudos, no sense of gratitude on their part or pleasure on yours.

By contrast, when you are free to choose whether to please God or not there is a wonderful liberty.

If we could but catch a glimpse of the glow of a church, special and loved in God's eyes, we would reconsider our own judgements.

Therefore, offer a prayer for the surviving remnant. 2 Kings 19:4b (CSB).

There is a better way to treat the CWASC. When we see God's necessary love for such a church, his own need to express his love for it, surely, we can do no other than to respond as he does. He leads the way. A CWASC does not need censure or condemnation, only prayer.

How easy is it to be a remnant? It is difficult to own it. We cannot have it both ways. To fight to be recognised as something – in this case a remnant - you must first own to being that thing. And particularly the minister. They must take a lead in this.

'My name is the Rev Robin Pritchard and I am the minister of a struggling church and I feel gutted that all my efforts bear such little fruit.' How releasing. So why do not we do it? Of course, I can say this safely now because I am retired from the front line. We are frightened to show weakness because we fear that if word gets out, we will not find sympathy, only censure. The surviving Remnant, and that includes the minster, needs prayer.

15 LORD God of Israel, you are righteous, for we survive as a remnant today. Ezra 9:15 (CSB).

Visitors used to comment on what a lovely atmosphere my previous parish church had and I would agree with them. I would tell them it was because the very walls were soaked in the prayers of countless generations of Christians over hundreds of years. I can see now that I was wrong to make that assertion. I acknowledge that it was not only because of the prayers of the Christians who historically met there, but also because of its present congregation. In a field on the end of my own parish were the remains of an old church. I visited it on a few occasions. Apart from the sense you get of history, I detected no atmosphere of worship. It had worn away – I do not know how long it took. I am not sure anybody came to pray there except me. The glory had departed, Ichabod, because it had no congregation.

If any church retains an atmosphere, it can only be because it has a live, if infrequent, congregation of faithful Christians who worship there and who leave the odour of the incense of their prayers behind.
[4] But what was God's answer to him? I have left seven thousand for myself who have not bowed down to Baal.
[5] In the same way, then, there is also at the present time a remnant chosen by grace. [6] Now if by grace, then it is not by works; otherwise grace ceases to be grace.
Romans 11:4-6 (CSB).

Paul reminds the Romans of Elijah's anguish that he has been left to fight God's battles on his own and how God answers and tells him of the seven thousand who remain who have not bowed down to Baal.

So, in our CWASCs we need to constantly reiterate our raison d'etre. It is only by grace that such churches may exist and fulfil God's purpose. Is it God's purpose that churches always grow year by year as in the world of consumerism? Should churches constantly get bigger, show increased profits? Is the hiddenness about being a Remnant important? If Elijah, one of the most spiritual of men, had no idea that these seven thousand existed, how can we lesser mortals hope to see what is going on? How had they managed to be so elusive and not draw attention to themselves. We have noted already that God sees the heart and not the outside. I repeat:
[4] But what was God's answer to him? I have left seven thousand for myself who have not bowed down to Baal.
Romans 11:4 (CSB).

There appears to be something quite mysterious about this Remnant. They are a group, reserved by God to be anonymous and secret in the world, in the parish of the

CWASC. How do they overlap with the congregation? This is so intriguing, yet Scripture offers very few answers currently.

In a rather ambiguous passage entitled 'Woe to Samaria' and decrying the drunkards of Ephraim comes this rather ambiguous verse: [5] **On that day the LORD of Armies will become a crown of beauty and a diadem of splendor to the remnant of his people,** Isaiah 28:5 (CSB).

In the introduction to my book *Honey from the Rock* I speak of the practice of mining the Bible for such unusual verses which are like finding detritus on a beach above the water line. Then like a beach comber reaping them, reusing them to a different purpose. This vague Remnant that may stretch beyond the walls of a CWASC, this cloud of witnesses both in the church and in the community around, show that the walls of a church are porous. How can we recognise them if they exist so circumspectly? They are a clear indication that we would do well not simply to count those who appear within the building when we assess a CWASC.

There is also a calumny against the Remnant. From Micah: **I will make the lame into a remnant,** Micah 4:7 (CSB).

Why is everyone so old in church people ask. Answers: To preserve and promote it as a holy space. To be caretakers. Old age is the piece of cloth at the end of the roll. The last bit of life. Not large enough for a whole garment, yet a dedicated seamstress may make something of it. And if she, why not God? It is easy to see witness as no more than a transfer of knowledge; the old as a repository of history. Yet the true mark of a Remnant is to follow God and give him honour.

Most keen sewers have a bag of remnants. Many get several inspections before any use is found for them; some are greeted like long lost friends. If they were able to feel trauma they might say: [12] **I am forgotten: gone from memory like a dead person—like broken pottery.** Psalms 31:12 (CSB).

In the end, very few are ever discarded. They are kept against the day when their best use is revealed.

CHAPTER 5 - Many Small V One Large.

[27] When the boys grew up, Esau became an expert hunter, an outdoorsman, but Jacob was a quiet man who stayed at home. Gen 25:27 (CSB).

Does God love a CWALC more or less than a CWASC? Well, he does not appear to do either. Although, as we see in the letters to the churches from the Book of Revelation, God remains aware of each church's failure, vulnerabilities and temptations, he has clearly retained a particular affection for the weak and vulnerable. As we have seen in the previous chapter God carries a particular torch for the Remnant. When we look back over church history, we can see the peaks and troughs of revival and strategic retreat. If you feel that as a church you are on the down it is terrifying to think you can be swept completely away. I do not believe that, although churches locally and nationally shrink and suffer the vagaries of God's emotions, they are ever brought to nothing. The exile in Babylon is an object lesson as to how God can lose patience and give up, or seemingly give up. Seventy years is a lifetime for many and for those who expired in exile it seemed like the end. Yet even the great exile in Babylon ended and in Nehemiah we read the wonderful, emotive story of Ezra. After many of the Hebrews have returned to Jerusalem, Ezra, at the people's request, reads out aloud the law to them - provoking tears of frustration and pain. Then we watch as the teaching of the 13 Levites bring them back to joy.

Here and there we find other glimpses in Scripture that reassure the CWASC that they have not only a special place in God's heart, but also work to do:

[17] Samuel continued, "Although you once considered yourself unimportant, have not you become the leader of the tribes of Israel? The LORD anointed you king over Israel... 1 Samuel 15:17 (CSB).

The CWALC is no less loved, but its temptations to be proud are greater and so are the consequences: **[62] Though you were as numerous as the stars of the sky, you will be left with only a few people, because you did not obey the LORD your God.** Deuteronomy 28:62 (CSB)

The large must find creative ways to deal with the effect of their influence: **[15] "If you have so many people," Joshua replied to them, "go to the forest and clear an area for yourselves there in the land of the Perizzites and the Rephaim, because Ephraim's hill country is too small for you."** Josh 17:15 (CSB).

I was, as you will have guessed, the priest of a CWASC for many years in my ministry. A CWALC, rather presumptuously, without engaging with us, decided that we were not really doing our job properly. That was an assumption – they never spoke to us. What they decided to do was to plant a church in the upper reaches of our parish to do a great work there. This felt so wrong in so many hurtful ways that I can still summon strong feelings about it many years later. Their rationale came from, I suspect, this wrong assumption that a CWASC means small, weak, failing and vulnerable, and so needed fixing. This is not how we perceived it or, fortunately, the diocese. I do not think anyone on my PCC would have rejected kindly, supportive help, or even feet on the ground to help us in our large parish. It was the arrogance that was so hard to stomach. If a church really is too large perhaps it needs to consider this sage advice to clear an area for themselves. Their intervention was unfortunately paternalistic. As it happened, we had our own plans for this area, not least in praying for a Church Army Officer to move into the estate.

[10] **Place no trust in oppression, or false hope in robbery. If wealth increases, do not set your heart on it**. Psalms 62:10 (CSB).

One of the major changes that affected my church was what our diocese called TRIO [The Responsibility Is Ours]. Although it was necessary to find a solution for stemming the haemorrhage of money in the diocese, it felt to me that it came hard on the heels of a grumbling from larger evangelical churches, who used their might nationally to fire a warning shot across the bows of dioceses. They wanted to establish a more congregational model for the church of England. They voiced specific complaints that they resented paying over large amounts of their money to their diocese, through the parish share, money that they felt better able to spend themselves with more returns. They believed that the dioceses, through this levy, were supporting churches that were small and failing, with ministries that were not, to them, theologically sound or fruitful.

It was another part of the creeping commercial model of church government. And it carried with it the whiff that money and success always have, namely, that we achieved this on our own and others who are not equally successful must be spiritual failures and ripe for condemnation. This is so against the spirit of the Scripture to be breath-taking. And its root lies at the heart of some many other cruel initiatives and is at the heart of the patriarchal system, racism and poor attitudes to addiction and disability. To my mind none of these have a part in the church. It is the Nebuchadnezzarian principle that presaged his descent into madness: I did this all myself. The CWALCs need to be particularly on their guard against it.

49 **Now this was the iniquity of your sister Sodom: she and her daughters had pride, plenty of food, and comfortable security, but did not support the poor and needy.** Ezek 16:49 (CSB).

I believe it is the responsibility of CWALCs to support the financially vulnerable churches with compassion and non-judgment. God judges by the heart and not by appearance.

18 **The prince must not take any of the people's inheritance, evicting them from their property. He is to provide an inheritance for his sons from his own property, so that none of My people will be displaced from his own property."** Ezek 46:18 (CSB).

I can't stress this enough - a CWASC is not necessarily so because it has done anything wrong. It may be that God has withheld his hand and not gifted it with the sort of people that can make much difference other than for it to survive; or it may simply be that in the same way a farmer with a very rock field, thus full of poor soil, a factor out of his control, will only produce a modest harvest compared to what they might have achieved with greater resources.

[5] **By your great skill in trading you have increased your wealth, but your heart has become proud because of your wealth."** Ezek 28:5 (CSB).

The CWALCs are called to humility about their success. Of course, it is down to hard work, but it is mostly down to God's work and blessing. Praise him.

[15] **This is the self–assured city that lives in security, that thinks to herself: I am, and there is no one besides me. What a desolation she has become, a place for wild animals to lie down! Everyone who passes by her jeers and shakes his fist.** Zeph 2:15 (HCSB).

Scripture clearly warns of the dangers of pride especially pride based on numbers and wealth. This is the unlovely side of superiority. Rather:

[10] **If he takes an additional wife, he must not reduce the food, clothing, or marital rights of the first wife.** Ex 21:10 (CSB).

The general differences between the CWASCs and the CWALCs are something to rejoice about and be encouraged by - for Scripture does not see such differences as a problem.

[27] **When the boys grew up, Esau became an expert hunter, an outdoorsman, but Jacob was a quiet man who stayed at home.** Gen 25:27 (CSB).

Our mighty God is a Lord that creates and thus celebrates different personalities, sizes, strengths and interests.

[17] **Do not show partiality when deciding a case; listen to small and great alike. Do not be intimidated by anyone, for judgment belongs to God. Bring me any case too difficult for you, and I will hear it**. Deuteronomy 1:17 (CSB).

Will God not take his own advice? And most particularly:

[24] **Who can agree to your proposal? The share of the one who goes into battle is to be the same as the share of the one who remains with the supplies. They will share equally."** [25] **And it has been so from that day forward. David established this policy as a law and an ordinance for Israel and it continues to this very day.** 1 Sam 30:24-25 (CSB).

Will not God be just to all churches and give fair shares?

CHAPTER 6 – Never Enough: The Limits Of Resources.

[14] **My brothers and sisters, I myself am convinced about you that you also are full of goodness, filled with all knowledge, and able to instruct one another.** Romans 15:14 (CSB).

Is it possible that when Paul speaks of God gifting the church, and even lists some of the possible ministries that God gives, he expected that every potential ministry would be present in every single church? If we accept that some churches may be very limited in total NUMBERS, does that mean there is some divine principle by which, as the number of participants reduces, so the number of ministries increases for everyone. That makes no logical sense. He must be talking about these gifts being present in the Church Universal rather than the Church Local. How then does a CWASC access them?

May it ask another church, 'Can I borrow your evangelist for a while?'

Why not?

'We could do with some deeper teaching than our own minister can provide. Can we have yours for a while? Well pay you back if you like. We've got a really good pastor here, with only a few miles on the clock, who will give sterling service for years to come.'

When Paul bewails his thorn in the flesh and his other weaknesses, he is given short shrift by God. The Lord's grace is sufficient for him. Is this not a metaphor for anybody, even a church body? A scary vision proposes itself of mutilated bodies strewn around a nation: here a body with no legs; here no hands; here a church without a local head.

Perhaps a church cannot get a new minister and they are three years into an interregnum. At this point, the diocese, like some Dr. Frankenstein, stitches several parishes together into a benefice hoping they can vivify the newly created cadaver.

In order to overcome such shortages, we find in Paul's ministry that when he moved on, he left behind experienced ministers to carry on the work of building up the congregation. He loaned them for a while. They were, presumably, attempting to make themselves redundant by helping newly formed congregations find their own expressions of giftedness. Even so there will be famines of specialist ministries. Times of famine may even be extended when a CWASC really does not have the right person to do the work.

We find these matters addressed in the Scriptures. For example, we learn that some people have a gift of healing. Then we discover that if someone is sick and no such a person is present, as an alternative, they are to call on the elders. We are not told what the consequence of these two different ministries are. Is the one with a gift more successful, or do the elders, aware of their own weakness and God's largesse, accomplish the same result? If we take a forensic accounting and auditing view of church life, we are bound to be disappointed.

Churches of all sizes are messy – we did not need to invent Messy Church, it already exists. I think we can only conclude that God did not expect for every congregation to have the full spectrum of available gifts and, that somehow, their lack manifests the grace of God in a church more clearly than if they had the full compliment. I have already alluded to the solution of sharing. Yet we all know it is not that simple. Some dioceses have tried to get around the natural tribalism that arises when such a suggestion is made by jointly hiring a Church Army Officer as an evangelistic resource for the whole deanery. Nevertheless, this does not address the root of the problem - we do not like to share. We never feel, however large a congregation we are, that we have enough members and gifted leaders to freely share our resources.

'Sorry, we would like to help but you must understand that it would limit our own work here.'

Resources are, or seem to be, too valuable to share. And you only need to add to this paternalistic attitude of one church to another, the temptation to judgmentalism I have mentioned, and you have a situation where the one with more wants to take over the other because they do not feel they are a worthy recipient of one of their precious resources.

In a recent movie the father of the household decided to sell their family holiday home to divide the money among his children.

To one he said, 'There, you now have sufficient money to go to college at last.'

The young man turned around and replied, 'Well since it is a gift and the implication is, I can do what I want with it, I will go around Europe with my girlfriend instead.'

A look of horror creeps over the father's face. His wonderful sacrifice - he really enjoyed his holiday home - will not be spent as he desired. He is filled with regrets. If we give money, time or talents to another church they may not feel it right to use it in the way we intended. A gift is a gift after all. As soon as it leaves our hand, we lose control. Such strong feelings seem to bedevil initiatives for churches to work together and most retreat in the Church of England behind their parish boundaries.

We think, 'If I send my young people to your CWALC, and its well-established youth work, they will never come back. Then we will effectively become an old-person church with no youth work.' Horror.

What inevitably happens, like the fact the water runs downhill by gravity, is that your young people, so desperately hung onto, subject to services that call themselves All-Age, but are by name only, naturally gravitate to a church that has bountiful youth work and you lose them anyway. And now with your reluctance and bad feeling towards the church who stole them, there is a bad smell in the air, a breaking of fellowship between churches. God loves a generous giver – I am talking about giving the best to the young people, not the other church. What would happen if you gave your young people away and sent them with your blessing to a place where they might find Christ. Who loses then?

It is incredibly sad when a church has finally to admit that it has no children's or young people's work. After years of trying every which way, the bullet must be bitten – they have gone. Does this mean the end of church as we know it? It should not. Of course, we are allowed to mourn for a bit, but then we must pick ourselves up and start again. Paul was stopped on several occasions carrying out his plans. That was the problem - they were *his* plans. Our prayer should change from, 'Oh Lord give us our children back,' to, 'What's your plan now Lord? Show us please so we can join in.'

I imagine one of the things we are likely to hear from him is, 'Seek you first the Kingdom of God.' This is always the best place to start. Children and young people in a church have unfortunately become a modern barometer to indicate church health, despite the adolescent and sometimes fickleness of the young, who like a swarm of bees, move on to a different church, when the fancy takes them, because it has better nectar. If a CWASC is not defined by numerical limits neither, should age define it.

Of course, these are obstacles, but none are beyond God to overcome if he wishes. We need to start measuring the health of a church by a completely different set of indicators. In the old days a person's spiritual health and worth, measured by entry into confirmation, was based on their knowledge of the catechism. If they could recite the questions and answers they were accepted. In today's world measuring spiritual health and maturity is obviously more than that. Perhaps then we need to move to a situation where the diocesan statistics do not solely show parish share paid but have some indices for Christian faithfulness, etc.

The verses - [14] **My brothers and sisters, I myself am convinced about you that you also are full of goodness, filled with all knowledge, and able to instruct one another.** [15] **Nevertheless, I have written to remind you more boldly on some points because of the grace given me by God.** Romans 15:14-15 (CSB). - seem to give an insight into Paul's confidence in the Roman church. How did he know this? Was it just flannel? Did he know that people do better when you praise them? Notice that having given them this remarkable testimonial he seems to take it back. The words - full **of goodness, filled with all knowledge, and able to instruct one another.** - are pregnant ones. Then Paul tells them, 'You still have a long way to go, nevertheless, you have made a good start.

How than can we build up the confidence of a CWASC? Here is a verse from Job:

14 He named his first daughter Jemimah, his second Keziah, and his third Keren-happuch. 15 No women as beautiful as Job's daughters could be found in all the land, and their father granted them an inheritance with their brothers. Job 42:14-15 (CSB).

After all Job's suffering and his complete capitulation to God everything is restored to him and more. With this largesse, he can make a startling and generous bequest in his will: he included his daughters in the inheritance. Woman at the time, and it is thought that Job is one of the earliest books of the Bible, were little more than chattels. They endure far worse iniquities than the CWASC, whose suffering is largely verbal and misunderstanding, and not the violence and sexual abuse of these historic women. These daughters of Job were unusually liberated into thinking that they were as worthy as their more powerful and privileged brothers. It enabled them to flourish, to marry well, and presumably for love, hopefully.

I wonder if you have ever visited a light house and gone up to see the mechanism? The light itself does not turn, but uniquely shaped screens rotate around it giving the distinct impression, from a distance, that the light is turning. It is this distinctive pattern of flashes that allows mariners to recognise which lighthouse it is. Between the beams of light there are periods of darkness. The light does not go out in the dark periods, it simply does not shine out. In the darkness the mechanism turns waiting for the opportunity to shine out.

The branch of Christianity that is triumphalist suggests that a church's progress should be like a sales chart, with year-on-year increase in profits. It is at our peril that we take commercial indicators to discern growth in churches. I have seen pictures of my previous church's building from the past where it seemed to be on the point of falling down. I have seen photographs of amazing congregations, between the wars, and the multiplicity of social events they promoted. My own ministry coincided with growing indifference in society towards the church and hence falling numbers. I will address the thorny question of whether I failed later in the book.

Nevertheless, if you chart Christianity's popularity over years, and even within your own parish, you will see it is more like a lighthouse than a sales chart. When we see some of the CWASC that we know were once large and flourishing, it is easy to be critical, particularly if your own church is shining out like a beacon for a few seconds. Please spare a thought for the poor church who finds its influence, its light, shut out by the screen, even as the mechanism turns in real time, for years perhaps. Is God the screen? Is it possible that God may continue to reveal himself to a church, but screen the effect for everyone else?

I was in my previous parish for 26 years and during that time I watched as my neighbouring churches waxed and waned in popularity as new ministers came and church goers left neighbouring churches to see what the new person had to offer. Some churches' congregations swelled and others declined. However, this was often due to transfer rather than new growth or fundamental inadequacy.

Perhaps a CWASC is not failing, but only taking its time as God's purposes roll around. If a church were universally successful all the time and full to the brim of every possible ministry, what would that say? Cannot God ring the changes if he wants to? How much influence do we really have to make any church successful, even with every resource? God measures what enough is. Paul learnt when he asked for more - The Lord's grace was sufficient for him.

Does not God's rain of blessing rain when God wants it and who are we are to argue if a drought appears. But come the day which we cannot see and [4] **You will no longer be called Deserted, and your land will not be called Desolate; instead, you will be called My Delight is in Her, and your land Married; for the LORD delights in you, and your land will be married.** [12] **And they will be called the Holy People, the LORD's Redeemed; and you will be called Cared For, A City Not Deserted.** Isaiah 62:4-12 (HCSB).

SECTION B – ITS STRENGTHS, GIFTS AND TESTS

CHAPTER 7 - It is Confidence In God's Promises.

[12] **A king's rage is like the roaring of a lion, but his favor is like dew on the grass.** Proverbs 19:12 (CSB).

We need to begin by planning how to use scriptural metaphors. Is for example a metaphor, which appears to be addressed to an individual, only to be applied to individuals; or one directed at Israel only to be appropriated by Israel; or can a metaphor that speaks of God's favour to an individual or Israel also be used to describe God's beneficence to a church, even a CWASC?

[5] **I will be like the dew to Israel; he will blossom like the lily and take root like the cedars of Lebanon.** Hosea 14:5 (CSB).

May God also be like the dew to a CWASC as well as Israel? We discover that the blessing given to Jacob, when he was masquerading as Esau, even when the deceit is discovered, remains. Does not such a theory of the transmission and appropriation of a blessing apply to a CWASC? I am going to say, 'Yes.'

I cannot believe that God, having watched us trawl through the Bible looking for verses to give us confidence in our lives, roles and ministries, and then finding one which, though not specifically directed to us, and yet finding comfort in it, would then forbid us from using it for ourselves. The true God who loves me and any CWASC will surely rejoice that we have turned to Scripture for solace anyway.

Where else can a CWASC look, if it is not in the Word of God, to find its purpose and the reassurance that whatever its size or reach of success, God loves it truly? To gain assurance, we must be confident enough in the first place to turn to Scripture.

So how do we respond when we see a church struggling to exist in a small rural village or a rundown town centre? Mindful of the disproportionate size of its building to congregation and the financial burden it has become; yet nurtured by a repository of dreams, as yet unfillable, with some historical spiritual memory of its glory days; looking around itself and seeing a few elderly people left, aged in years and attitude, but who, if faced with quiet and polite questioning, will reveal a deep faith in Jesus, yet struggling in confidence - when they want to know if there is any hope for them? There is hope the Scripture assures us. We find first a slew of verses:

21 **Blessed be the LORD, for he has wondrously shown his faithful love to me in a city under siege.** Psalms 31:21 (CSB).

1 **God is our refuge and strength, a helper who is always found in times of trouble.** Psalms 46:1 (CSB).

11 **The LORD values those who fear him, those who put their hope in his faithful love.** Psalms 147:11 (CSB).

My dwelling place will be with them; I will be their God, and they will be my people. Ezek 37:27 (CSB).

And in 23 **There is profit in all hard work,** Prov 14:23a (CSB), we find that all things that are done in the name of God and for him will bear fruit.

These verses reveal God's love is not a reaction to success, but a response to his love. God loves because he can and he wills to. Personal strengths and qualities are of no consequence.

Despite what the CWASCs see and feel God remains with the poor in spirit, not as a response to their faith, however weak it may be, but because he is Yahweh. God has will, power and intention. He has his ways and his plans, and the present state of the churches I have described, will not scupper them. That does not mean he might not show some new initiative or bring in people with fresh energy. I do not think it means he will abandon any of his faithful, however down the scale of human or ecclesiastical success they seem to have sunk.

Neither does that mean that God thinks they are so far on the scrap heap that he has no expectations of them. Nobody is too old for these things; nobody exempt from them. God's graceful love is also God's direct challenge. When we are truly loved for what we are, so we may be challenged hard to be what he wants us to be.

So, we find our second list, this time of challenges:
[20] **Pursue justice and justice alone, so that you will live and possess the land the LORD your God is giving you.** Deut 16:20 (CSB).

The CWASC is to pursue justice. Is the congregation too old, too troubled or too distracted for direct action? Then let them pray. At least let them decline to be involved in injustice. Let them say, 'No.'

When Elijah complained to God that he was the only one left God told him directly, and we do not know from the passage what tone of voice he uses – consolatory, angry or cajoling - that there are seven thousand left who had not bowed the knee to Baal. Elijah could not see them. Their action seemed of so little consequence that it was unobservable. Yet God saw them. They were not far along enough to acknowledge God or perhaps even to bow the knee to him, but their rejection of Baal, by refusing to submit, was positive action enough to attract God's attention. If we can do nothing else then at least we can refuse to bow the knee to injustice. If only we could see how much credence and delight God places on the smallest, most insignificant gesture in his direction, we would be humbled by our lack of compassion and the ease to which we jump to judgment. And see the reward – such people will possess the land.

[9] **"The LORD of Hosts says this: Render true justice. Show faithful love and compassion to one another.** Zech 7:9 (HCSB).

We are called to show faithful love and compassion to one another.

Even this apparently small act in our sight is huge in God's. God will love a CWASC for it. God will love them for the Fairtrade stall or poster in the damp porch of the church. We are too easily dissatisfied with the efforts other people make and wish to consign them to the failure bin, fortunately God starts lower down.

[20] **Keep my Sabbaths holy, and they will be a sign between me and you, so you may know that I am the LORD your God."** Ezekiel 20:20 (CSB).

Some CWASCs faithfully ensure they have the statutory HC service once a Sunday, where even small numbers gather to sustain the continuing practice of true religion. They worship and proclaim their wonderful God and his sacrifice, they repent and receive forgiveness, they read Scripture and hear a homily, they partake of the Eucharistic meal and receive the blessing before going home. As small and as boring as this may seem, intoned with dry, dusty, old voices, poor intentions and trouble minds, nevertheless, what they do counts as faithfulness. See how the wrong criterion of success pollutes how we gauge and value endeavours other than our own. 'Dear, dear, dreary me,' we might think. Yet let us be taken back and remind ourselves that it is not our opinion, but God's that counts. Is there a smile or a frown on God's face when he sees such old dry sticks looking for a rekindling by the Holy Spirit? Does he enjoy himself more in a slick, modern worship service with enthusiastic young people raising their hands in glory? Or might he enjoy both? Where does he feel himself more honoured? Is God bothered by such differences? If the smallest seed of faith can raise a mighty tree, we might find that the difference between these two services that seem to be separated by an enormous distance in our mind seem no more than the distance between Canterbury and York when God looks from the other side of the immensity of space in a galaxy far away. We have developed an idolatrous vision of comparison which is based on human scale and not God's.

The acid test is who knows **that I am the LORD your God."** Ezekiel 20:20 (CSB).

28 **"This will be their inheritance: I am their inheritance. You are to give them no possession in Israel: I am their possession.** Ezek 44:28 (CSB).

The CWASC have an object lesson in their experience of retreat: not only their faculties and their diminishing physical strength, if the congregation is old, but the obvious fact that their building needs more care than they can give it. They sense ultimately that they can take nothing with them. What they have is what they are. They will not pass that way again. All this sage wisdom is so readily rejected by the immature, but length of years brings understanding of realities denied the young in their mistaken invincibility. What at the end of the day do you possess which you can take with you? The only thing that goes with you is that the God you loved, adored and worshipped in the world, you will also find in the next. Hosanna. Who needs anything else when this is true? Maybe church buildings do not matter as much. It is good to travel light and keep reviewing how we journey. If God is to be our overall then who we are, whether we be a CWASC or CWALC ceases to matter at all.

However, let us not get unnecessarily maudlin. I am writing this for the church now, to those who will listen to what I am saying about the value of the CWASC and how not to denigrate it.

For I am jealous over you with a Godly jealousy, because I have promised you in marriage to one husband—to present a pure virgin to Christ. 2 Cor 11:2 (CSB).

Q. Why should not a CWASC be free of fear? A. With God nothing is impossible.

It amazed me throughout my ministry that when I met a couple for the first time, when they arrived at my rectory to book a wedding, as to how ill matched, they seemed to be. What a wonderful gift that God has given that very often the most unpromising of people can find somebody to love them. One of God's great plans is to produce a bride for his son. The Church Universal is to be Jesus' bride and in the ambiguity of metaphors that also means that my church, my CWASC, is also part of this romance. For in its separateness and uniqueness, it also finds shelter under the umbrella of being a bride of Christ. Something that both the CWASC and the CWALC hold in common is that they are brides and part of the bride of Christ. Husbands generally think that their brides are the loveliest person they know. Marriage has such a powerful effect because it is a public statement of love.

I remember one lovely couple, early on in my ministry who unusually, later in life, found each other. Most noticeable was how both blossomed so remarkably due to the love of the other, to the extent that they appeared to become quite different people. At the end of the day confidence comes about by being loved and knowing it. Is a CWASC a poor bride for God, a mail order bride for the man who can't attract his own? Oh no!!Does God love the CWASC as much as the CWALC? Oh yes!! Such are the effects of God's promises.

It is worth saying at this stage in the book that God does not have rose-tinted spectacles. Are all CWALC as bad as the examples I give? Of course not. Neither are all the CWASC as virtuous or good as they might be.

CHAPTER 8 – God's Dew.

In previous chapters I alluded to the spiritual metaphor of dew. It is time to pursue this briefly. God's kindness, beneficence and generosity is exemplified by dew. There are clearly scientific meteorological conditions that make one place rather than another experience dew. It needs to reach the dew point [condensation] to appear.

12 **A king's rage is like the roaring of a lion, but his favor is like dew on the grass.** Proverbs 19:12 (CSB).

I like looking at dew, yet find it an awful nuisance if I must walk over dew laden grass with unsuitable shoes. It is easy to get drenched and end up with wet feet. I forget so easily - the dew is not really for me. I personally do not benefit from dew. The dew is for the world in which I inhabit. It is for my garden and the crops we eat. Of course, it is all to do with atmospheric temperature and humidity, but so what. This is a metaphor for goodness' sake.

I realise writing this that I have never tried to drink dew. Perhaps I shall try it and report back later in the book?

It is not about dew, it is about God's favour which is like dew. When dew forms it blankets everything. It is all encompassing and generous to a fault. It is infinitely to be preferred to the king's rage, to King Jesus' rage, which is more like a roaring lion. I know which I want.

Does the dew, like the rain, fall on the just and unjust? Well, yes, because that's God's providence.

Mmm. I begin to ramble, 'It is God's favour. Favour as in favourite. God may favour me and not someone else. His rain rains on all. See, God loves me, he tells me I am his favourite.' I hope you are smiling here at my naivety. Children think like that do not they? Some metaphors are not exponentially and continuously applicable. The dew dries up when the sun comes out. Yet, what else will give a church confidence other than the memory of God's love when it has dried up. We had dew today, we might have it tomorrow or next week. It will come again I know.

Dew seems to have a less vigorous purpose than rain, even gentle rain. It is ephemeral and does not hang about. Dew is more associated with spiritual blessings. Dew, it appears, is a metaphor for the king's favour.

12 **A king's... favor is like dew on the grass.** Proverbs 19:12 (CSB).

In what sense then does a CWASC, in this incidence, experience the king's favour, the favour of the High God of Heaven? As with all metaphors in Scripture they occupy mixed ground. They do not have a homogenous interpretation. Dew may indeed be the king's favour, but it is also an image of the transient nature of God's chosen people and of God's chosen church. The security for a church is not dependent on its own self-consciousness or its own energy or ability to survive. All may be lost in a moment if God's favour is withdrawn.

3 **Therefore, they will be like the morning mist, like the early dew that vanishes, like chaff blown from a threshing floor, or like smoke from a window.** Hosea 13:3 (CSB).

This does not make God capricious. It strengthens the argument that God is in absolute control and his favour rests on his own cognizance, on his own decisions to bestow it, and that his decision-making process is only as clear as he makes it and as is as obscure as he is inscrutable.

In the previous chapter we dealt with the CWASC as a remnant and now we find a direct link between that image and this puzzling one of dew:

7 Then the remnant of Jacob will be among many peoples like dew from the LORD, like showers on the grass, which do not wait for anyone or linger for mankind. Micah 5:7 (CSB).

Dew is not only illusive, but difficult to pin down as it flits from a metaphor for protagonist to antagonist; to substance; to a blessing from God; to the people themselves as being like the blessing of dew. When things go well then, the dew can even be turned from water to wine so to speak.

19 Your dead shall live, their corpses shall rise. O dwellers in the dust, awake and sing for joy! For your dew is a radiant dew, and the earth will give birth to those long dead. Isaiah 26:19 (NRSV).

Radiant dew or 'morning dew' as the HSBC translates it.

5 I will be like the dew to Israel; he will blossom like the lily and take root like the cedars of Lebanon. 6 His new branches will spread, and his splendor will be like the olive tree, his fragrance, like the forest of Lebanon. Hosea 14:5-6 (CSB).

If a CWASC is to grow and thrive to be like the splendour of an olive tree, fragrant, like the trees of the forest of Lebanon, it can only be at God's direction. There are no human endeavours in this. At best we are co-workers and neither are large numbers involved: the allusion to dew on Gideon's fleece resulted in him listening to God and ditching his huge army. Worryingly, God insists he takes a very paired down one to defeat the enemy. Thus, courting the possibility that too few soldiers will not be sufficient for the already unmanageable circumstances. Where have we heard that before?

CHAPTER 9 – Measuring Success In A CWASC

[28] **"For this is what the Lord GOD says: I am going to hand you over to those you hate, to those you turned away from in disgust.** Ezek 23:28 (CSB).

All churches fail when they do not follow God. Their numerical strength – small, medium or large – is no defence.

So, rather than judging by success maybe the best way to categorise churches is by their failure. In fact, a reading of all of Scripture according to Failism [I have invented that word] is quite an edifying experience. The internet has many examples of compilations of 'fails'. There are short clips of people making a complete fool of themselves: like trying to jump over a low rope and catching their foot on it so they fall flat on their face. At the end of each section a big rubber stamp comes and inks a large FAIL on the corner. A Failism reading of Scripture would go like this:

Man and woman ignore warning not to eat forbidden fruit. FAIL. Man murders his brother in fit of jealousy. FAIL. Tower to heaven falls short of its target when the builders get confused. FAIL. People of God give up waiting for Moses to return and go back to idol worship. FAIL. King David seduces the wife of one of his soldiers. FAIL. King David takes a census. FAIL. Israel murders its prophets. FAIL. Saul tries to exterminate Christians. FAIL. A Christian church does not censure a man for sleeping with his father's wife. FAIL. And so, it goes on. Surely, with such a great catalogue of failures in the Scripture it should encourage us to take heart. Any church, whether a

CWASC or a CWALC, can hold its head up high in such exalted and exemplary company!

Yet out of each of those historic fails something good comes. Maybe the measure is not that we fail, but how we respond to it? This leads us to consider that it is not how we succeed, but how we respond to triumph.

If I have not yet convinced you that we should measure any Christian enterprise, not solely from the outside and not only with human judgement, but on the inside as God sees, then what else can I say?

It is time to move forward on the assumption that there are far better ways to assess any situation, and particularly in this case the CWASC.

I believe it is now well past time to stop regarding success as a Christian virtue. We are in the world and not of it. The value system of the world is an inappropriate measuring stick. We need to find a new one.

How then does a CWASC see itself? That is a good point to start - with its own self-awareness. Perhaps, as you would with a person in a counselling situation, you need to create a timeline, a personal history, engaging with the older members of the congregation, to detail how the church got to this point in their pilgrimage. I know from my own church that a major schism, during which several people left, particularly some of the younger ones, those with specialist gifts and families with little children, had caused an effect for years to come. Going further back, it is still in living memory, in a similar way, the effects of the Second World War had on the congregation who lived through it. And they will share older memories with their parents of the First World War.

All this will have had an effect. We find other catalysts for these historic changes of the church such as: the results of the migration of young people out of the parish, urban planning, loss of local jobs due to industrialisation, of agriculture changes and in the congregational numbers of other local churches. No wonder the OT is full of reminders to pay attention to the back story of previous generations of the people of Israel at every moment in their present experience. These changes in the histories of our churches have all been things beyond the power of the present congregation to overcome. It is likely that they will feel guilty and discouraged by association, and feel they are held responsible for all its ills. As their numbers decreased and money followed suit, and ill matched vicars came, or they lost their own priest when they were beneficed; it became a tide that they could not withstand, despite their faith. Like the sea invading a fortified beach work, they are one last enclave that lives constantly with the danger of being swept away. They are vulnerable to infection by anti-Christian elements disproportionately and feel doubt and fear more strongly. All these factors cannot be ascribed to lack of faith or practice. In addition, the indifference and secularity of society is another enemy empire that tries to take them into exile; the secular forces in their own community and new-fangled ways of doing church [this being the voice of their own prejudiced judgement of course, which they must face and own up to!] do not sit easily with them, causing pain. It is so easy to see that, even with a determined effort on their part to walk back up this descending escalator, they will eventually be tipped onto the platform at the bottom.

That whole generation was also gathered to their ancestors. After them another generation rose up who

did not know the LORD or the works He had done for Israel. Judges 2:10 (CSB).

If there is any failure, something that can be laid at any church's door, it is this: the curse of the second-generation. I have a sense that Christian parents must own some responsibility when their own children fail to birth properly and instead carry on a shallow religion of outward forms. Should we feel sorry for them? I do not know the answer to this. I am a Christian parent myself and wrestle with the 'Are we to be blamed' question.

Perhaps God is responsible? It is easier to hold him liable. Where was he in our past history? The prophets of Church Growth and their insistence for year-on-year increase have not helped. The promoters of Kingdom Theology criticise such churches for not being more triumphalist... and excited... and upbeat... at the wonderful work God is doing, yet fail to acknowledge the small intense light that continues in the hearts of members of a CWASC.

However, I believe that the perilous nature of being a CWASC, in an inimical society, is one which can only be corrected if fellow Christians and churches affirm that the CWASC is more likely to succeed if they are reminded and encouraged by God's warm heart rather than his disapproval. My wife and I keep a bottle of Cava in the fridge and when we have some notable success, we celebrate with it as a way of encouraging ourselves. [11] **A city is built up by the blessing of the upright, but it is torn down by the mouth of the wicked.** Prov 11:11 (CSB).

When we have constructed our timeline, then is the chance for the therapist to draw out the interpretation and to help the church counselee to discover for themselves what has brought the present situation to pass. Some counsellors will be completely non-directive. However, I have always found counsellors who are prepared to give an opinion, if difficult to prize out of them, of value. Our therapist though is God. All this introspection has been a preparation for us to begin to ask his opinion. We have laid before him how we got to this point and we have acknowledged our part in it. We note though that even this self-analysis has been God directed through Scripture, for we are not very good at it and need his strong words to make us focus. Perhaps God will say:

4 You have not strengthened the weak, healed the sick, bandaged the injured, brought back the strays, or sought the lost. Ezek 34:4a (CSB).

Were we prepared for that? Did we see that coming – our own heart pain is the result of God's pain in our behaviour? For:

1 Unless the LORD builds a house, its builders labor over it in vain; unless the LORD watches over a city, the Night Guard stays alert in vain. Psalms 127:1 (CSB).

I hate wasting my time over anything and to be caught out by discovering that some church task I initiated was entirely from my own imagination, and I had not thoroughly checked it out with God enough to find out if he was in it, and then wasted my energy going stubbornly ahead anyway, makes my blood boil and fills me with self-pity. I was fascinated at school to learn about blocks and pulleys and how quite large weights could be shifted by such simple means. When we think of such simple mechanical machines we need to think – Yes - God is one of those. How easily he could move anything should he wish, how much he could multiply our weak power by the spiritual block and tackle of his approbation. Frequently, we waste all that effort by stupidly pushing back against God, going in the opposite direction.

These are such well-trodden scriptural references that it is easy to disregard them when they are read to us. Take:

[5] Trust in the LORD with all your heart, and do not rely on your own understanding; [6] in all your ways know him, and he will make your paths straight. Proverbs 3:5-6 (CSB).

This was at the heart of my failures described before. I relied on my own comprehension. I was foolish and not wise. Of course, I can admit it now, but it is not so easy when you are in it and you must have the courage to own up and reverse a decision.

[15] If anyone's work is burned up, it will be lost, but he will be saved; yet it will be like an escape through fire. 1 Corinthians 3:15 (CSB). Phew, if all our plans come to nothing, then at least we tried and we will survive due to God's mercy. Let us not underestimate the bottom line here: God's provision as a failsafe.

CHAPTER 10 - Age In A CWASC.

Old age is to be honoured. Elderly people have their place and a role in the fellowship.

[29] **He took his last breath and died, and was gathered to his people, old and full of days. His sons Esau and Jacob buried him.** Gen 35:29 (CSB).

[9] **Do not discard me in my old age: as my strength fails, do not abandon me.** Psalms 71:9 (CSB).

[29] **The glory of young men is their strength,**
and the splendor of old men is gray hair. Proverbs 20:29 (CSB).

[2] **Older men are to be self-controlled, worthy of respect, sensible, and sound in faith, love, and endurance.** [3] **In the same way, older women are to be reverent in behavior, not slanderers, not slaves to excessive drinking.** Titus 2:2,3 (CSB).

Old people, eh? CWASCs are often disproportionally represented by older people. They are seen as the last vestiges of life before the whole church kicks the bucket. They are portrayed as resistant to change, and are those church members who are not prepared to go somewhere else - ever. So, the meme runs. No wonder they evoke no sympathy when they are viewed as being the last obstacle before a church can be revitalised. They must embrace the new ways or they are out, we decide. Do they deserve such a judgment? Are they the generation responsible for bringing the church to its knees? Surely it is necessary for dry, old, liturgical services to be ended and let the younger generation give it a go? There is a generational fight going on in the church. And with young, trendy-looking clergy, who eschew the dog collar, trying to attract the 'yoof' generation by trying to be cool, we find an unstoppable force meeting an immovable object. And then there are those young people who, frankly, consider anybody beyond their own age as past it. Has something gone wrong with the church, the way of doing church, the old people? Or is it something to do with more fundamental reasons in society that project indifference to the church and little respect of elderly people, caused by short attention spans and the itchy ears of those who want a religion that does not present too many challenges, but makes them feel good?

It is worth remembering that God is old. Well, of course he never changes and, in that sense, he never ages, but old he remains in a historical way; always there from time before time, full of wisdom and love, ineffable. Would we do better with a young God, full to the brim with fresh ideas?

The real God treats us with love and respect, even when we do not treat each other with deference. Do young people respect the old enough and are the old so sour and cantankerous that they have driven the younger generation to anger? I note here the numerous occasions where grandchildren, attending the funerals of their grandparents, were deeply moved and sorrowful at their loss, even voluble in uncharacteristic teenage ways about the love they had received from them. The Bible's take on fathers/parents is a good one: adults should love their children and not drive them to anger, and children should honour and obey them back.

What does the Bible have to say about the treatment of the old, and why we should treat them well?

[2] "You are to rise in the presence of the elderly and honor the old. Fear your God; I am Yahweh. Leviticus 19:32 (CSB).

[12] Wisdom is found with the elderly,
and understanding comes with long life.
[13] Wisdom and strength belong to God;
counsel and understanding are His. Job 12:12-13 (CSB).

I will be the same until your old age,
and I will bear you up when you turn gray.
I have made you, and I will carry you;
I will bear and save you. Isaiah 46:4 (CSB).

Well, that is very clear. God does not hold the same opinion of older people that some do. In fact, they are to be treated with respect and honoured we are told; we should acknowledge that God cares for them and sees worth in them, and expects other people to treat them with respect and value their opinion. At least until they are a grumpy old sod! God's love and commitment are not at the expense of other people. God succours and supports the old, but that does not mean that they do not have responsibilities to match God's love with the reality of worthiness.

Old men and women have particular responsibilities in terms of their attitude. They may no longer have the physical vitality to make much of a contribution, yet they are a historical repository of lessons learned and distress overcome. Jeroboam, Solomon's son first took advice from his father Solomon's old counsellors and then, rejecting them, from his younger friends, thus bringing a long-lasting rift between Israel and Judah and split the kingdom that his father and grandfather has so carefully built up.

This does not mean that older people cannot be a rather difficult congregation to pastor. I remember numerous occasions when the generation of my parents caused me problems by their cruel pig-headedness. Paul's advice to Timothy rings true:

[1] **Do not rebuke an older man, but exhort him as a father, younger men as brothers,** [2] **older women as mothers, and with all propriety, the younger women as sisters.** 1 Timothy 5:1-2 (CSB).

Paul tells him: [12] **Do not let anyone despise your youth...** 1 Timothy 4:12a (CSB). And he means - managing the older members of the church.

When God talks so positively about the benefits of the older people, we older people need to listen.

God often phrases his narrative towards us as, 'I love you wholeheartedly and I will defend you. My love is so strong towards you. However, now you've really heard that you must behave yourselves, I am going to teach you how you should conduct yourself towards younger people and younger Christians.'

However, in this chapter we note that just because you are old does not mean you are in the right simply because you are old. Rather, it is more likely that these old people are right and deserve to be heard because they are still following God unreservedly and their faith is great. Make sure it shows!

It is interesting to note in Paul's letter to Philemon, where each word counts because of its brevity, that he tells Philemon he is old.

9 I appeal, instead, on the basis of love. I, Paul, as an elderly man and now also as a prisoner of Christ Jesus, Philem 1:9 (CSB).

He is not excusing himself. I believe this is a part of Paul's righteous boasting that appears scattered through his letters. Treat me as an example to emulate he pronounces.

'I am old and in prison, therefore listen to me. I have something important to say.' Philemon listens. Old people are not allowed to say, 'I am old, therefore listen to me in a selfish way.'

There is the meme of daughters staying at home and not getting married so enthralled are they by ageing parents that they are dominated and blackmailed by them.

'See, look how sick I am. You must stay with me. I cannot manage without you.' Tying a younger generation to our apron strings is not justice.

Old age and experience do not need to be proved to the sensible; they are obvious. 'Clearly, he knows what he is talking about,' we should think.

It is horrible growing old, knowing your body and your mind are fading slowly, having to pack your things in smaller and smaller boxes, as you can no longer lift the old ones. Let us pray to God:

Even when I am old and gray, God, do not abandon me. Then I will proclaim Your power to another generation, Your strength to all who are to come. Psalms 71:18 (CSB).

And God promising:

[2] The righteous thrive like a palm tree and grow like a cedar tree in Lebanon. [13] Planted in the house of the LORD, they thrive in the courts of our God. [14] They will still bear fruit in old age, healthy and green, [15] to declare: "The LORD is just; He is my rock, and there is no unrighteousness in Him." Psalms 92:12-15 (CSB).

We often cry, 'We have no young people in our church!' We are like Eeyore - our cup is half empty.

How about, 'Oh good, we have some older, committed Christians in the church. See how they have managed to hang on and at least preserve this building hoping it will be full once again.' In my experience most older people rejoice when somebody young turns up in their church and are sensible enough to know that change must occur. They expect to make sacrifices, even though they do not wish to, or even believe that some of these changes will work. A long life has taught them that.

However, it is right and proper for fair shares. Churches should have a mixed economy; where nobody gets all they want, but everybody finds a little of something they like. Why does something new have to exclude something old? A good steward brings both old and new from his storehouse. There is real need for creative amelioration and the construction of a common mind. I knew of a PCC that would not make any change unless the vote for it was unanimous. What a challenge, we might declare and groan! Yet the incumbent told me that it made for good harmony and real progress.

In all three of my congregations most of the older people had lived through the war and been formed by their experiences of it. In the way that old soldiers often do not want to talk about their experiences in a battle, older Christians, who had to button up a lot of their emotions in the past, still find it hard to talk about their feelings, not just of the war, but also their faith. They remain shut down by a whole series of formative life experiences, not least growing up when children's opinions were not sought and often violently quelled. Yet I was privileged over the years eventually to hear from most of the elderly in the congregation, although never fulsomely, about how important Jesus was to them.

As part of the National Curriculum primary schools send children into old people's residential and nursing homes to hear some remembered history. With a little encouragement, something similar, can happen in churches to revive spiritual memories. In my own church an older single woman was able to recount how she responded and was converted at the Lowestoft Revival in the 1920s and consequently went abroad to Burma, as it was then known, as a missionary.

I am talking really about the active old here. The even older members, who have moved beyond church attendance into nursing and residential homes, are another matter and beyond this book. Their care and continuing nurture remains a challenge though.

We are really asking who is to blame when it comes to the present state of the church? Perhaps we should stop looking for a scapegoat. The scapegoat was allowed to wander free anyway! I believe it really is a conundrum of factors that has brought us to this place. With the fall in attendance at churches and all that we see about present church life, blaming any generation for its faults or embracing any generation uncritically for its solutions is to be avoided. Do we not think that the ancestors of our present churches did not worry about how their church was doing back in their day? Have we got some idea that they were some cavalier spendthrifts who did not care at all? Of course, they agonised. It may not even be anyone's fault anyway as we have seen from the analysis of the metaphor of the Remnant.

Maybe we need to face the possibility that God is not really calling many in this generation and he is allowing the message to be lost to the society we live in, even allowing it to run down to virtually nothing, until the country as a whole turns back to God and cries out for help. [The Judges cycle]. We just happen to be the suckers who feel all the guilt now.

There is nothing new under the sun the Scripture tells us. Over a long ministry I have lost count of how may new initiatives and conferences I have attended for church growth and how, even so, the decline continues. So many hopes for a national revival unfounded. We need to ask ourselves, once we have stopped blaming each other, whether we need to be censured instead because we have incorrectly imagined what we believe God wants at this time, without thoroughly asking him for fear we do not like the answer. Why are we so afraid to hear this?

Does it mean that God has given up on the remaining faithful few?

What happens if God says actually, 'I am not doing anything now.' And, 'It is like during the Exile, just hunker down and get on with life and remain faithful.'

D. Bonhoeffer in *No Rusty Swords says*: *It is not we who build. He wills to build the church. No man builds the church but Christ alone. Whoever is minded to build the church is surely on his way to destroying it; for he will build a temple to idols without wishing or knowing it. We must confess – he builds. We must proclaim – he builds. We must pray to him – he builds. We do not know his plan. We cannot see whether he is building or pulling down. It may be that the times which by human standards are times of collapse are for him the greatest times of building. It may be that the times which from a human point of view are great times for the church are times when it is pulled down. It is a great comfort which Christ gives to his church: you confess, preach, bear witness to me, and I alone will build where it pleases me.*

I have been at great pains to point out that a church is a church regardless of how many people, even old people, are in it. The same is true of the National Church too. This is not to pour cold water on any initiatives, but to be very careful how we approach them and to check whether they really are to God's glory and not our own. The wisdom of the old must also embrace the wisdom of the historical old. Perhaps now is the time to scrupulously search through Church and Salvation history to see how that might comment on the situation we are in, rather than short-term, knee-jerk reactions. Maybe the emphasis to attract the youth into church is itself misplaced, especially if it comes at the expense of mission to the elderly. When asked churches often want their new incumbent to be a young person with a family. What of old clergy? Where should we send somebody with years of experience? The mission to the elderly must take quite a different form. They are not taken in by novelty or fashion. The old need to be drawn in with as much expertise as the young.

CHAPTER 11 - Maybe Only Witnesses - And That Is Enough.

16 God made the two great lights—the greater light to have dominion over the day and the lesser light to have dominion over the night—as well as the stars. Genesis 1:16 (CSB).

God is wise. Of course, he is. For the sake of economy, we humans would have made one light and probably had it on all the time. But no, he will go his own way! He made two lights so as to separate day and night. There are ordinarily day time pursuits that need more light and nocturnal pursuits that need less. The strength and the length of the daily appearance of the sun in the sky also marks the different seasons. As the earth wings its yearly way further and then, like a boomerang, returns nearer to the sun, so it follows its predestined course. The moon waxes and wanes month by month.

Speaking for myself, the thing I hate most of all are ordinary, consistent things unchanging, going on and on. I find life boring when it is like that. Of course, when I am very busy, challenged by crisis, that is exactly what I want. God has accommodated the human personality by varying things slowly and slightly through the seasons and year by year. Each day is new every morning. Nature is resplendent in variety. So why should God make every church identical, when he rarely makes two humans the same? Why not make things appropriate for the age they are? Cannot institutions follow the path of human development, tracking from childhood innocence and curiosity, passing to burgeoning youthful fruitfulness, bearing the weight of families on their shoulders, then losing strength as limbs weaken and become arthritic, waning like the sun and finally basking in the gentle moonlight? What is so wrong with some churches being in the last stages of their lives? Do we really need to euthanise them before their time? There would be outrage if you did it with the older human population, who still have so much to offer. Why time out churches? Some churches are no longer ruled by the greater light, but by the softer lights of the night – moon and stars.

What are the qualities of a church that is moving from dusk to eventide, yet still illuminated by the softer light of God's presence in its nocturnal phase? It is good to note that moonlight is obviously reflected light, the moon has none of its own. It is almost as if the harsh glare of the sun, the full power of God's interest, is muted when brought to bear towards those who are of the night, those who require God's encouragement and not censure.

What are the things of moonlight in the life of a church?

11 to seek to lead a quiet life, to mind your own business, and to work with your own hands, as we commanded you, 1 Thess 4:11 (CSB).

It is quite difficult when you are first retired to slow down and stop, and particularly to forgo sticking your nose into things that no longer concern you. Especially if you are a clergyperson! I have sensed God putting his hand on my arm on a number of occasions as much to say, 'Whoa. Stop! Not your business anymore.'

This raises the question as to whether a church might retire. One of my principles, when I was an incumbent, was to make sure that all age groups and tastes were catered for.

I used to tell people when they complained about change or things that they did not like, 'Well, I hope that you will find something you like in the variety we provide, but you cannot expect to find everything to your taste.'

In addition, the church ran special interest groups to cater for people's particular predilections and the ways they wanted to express their faith. This is an issue which I want to consider more deeply in the chapter about introverts and extroverts. The point I am trying to illustrate is that if we take the metaphor of the church being the body of Christ, we must develop that metaphor in its application as we think of the human life of a body throughout its life. And if we are willing to accept our own ageing then we must also accept that churches age and that interests change as well: that strength is lost; that wisdom and maturity hopefully increase. What is lost in physical stamina is compensated by other things. In the same way that you are not likely to find a slew of over 70s dancing the night away at a nightclub, you will not find one homogenous group of young people liking quieter more peaceful pursuits continuously. That surely is OK? It is the nature of things and ought to be accepted and applauded. Squeezing the life of a church into some sort of homogenous, monochrome experience, surely falls well short of the glory of the Saviour, and those churches in America that pursue such a high-return evangelism discipline programme, where everything is subordinated to this sausage machine of conversion, a travesty.

[11] **to seek to lead a quiet life, to mind your own business, and to work with your own hands, as we commanded you,** 1 Thess 4:11 (CSB).

Seems quite a nice thing. I am 68 though!

At the same time:

[39] For I tell you, you will never see Me again until you say, **Blessed is He who comes in the name of the Lord!**" Matthew 23:39 (CSB).

The old and frail are called to develop and continue in a deep and rich inner life. Their spirituality may not be so obvious to a cursory glance, but it should be obvious to a deeper look. Perhaps that is the problem - we do not look too carefully at churches. Diocesan return forms only seem to require numerical answers in terms of numbers and finances; baptisms, weddings, funerals, average attendance and attendance at the two major festivals; plus, of course, the dreaded AGM accounts – so complicated now they can only be compiled by an accountant!

Would it not be better if a proper review of a church required somebody to come and observe it, not simply a review of the clergy, but the whole church, which is a living thing – a body indeed? Presupposing we can find a way to measure spirituality, and being appropriately cautious of giving offence, why do not we do it? How ground-breaking it would be to interview the participants, and to detect and record some sort of quotient that indicated depth of spirituality. How wonderful to balance the statistics with some way of saying, 'Circumstances seem to have dictated that the church has none of the obvious numerical or financial markers of a church doing well, but essentially when you measure their faith, it is off the scale.' Faith often thrives and increases in adversity as opposed to sufficiency. Could it even be true to say that the churches that are struggling the most are the more spiritual? The Apostle Paul seems to be at his most reassuring and encouraging at the moment of his greatest failure and need. Is the quiet peace of the dying man, fully assured of where he is going, as he faces the ultimate test of his faith, less or more than the faith of a younger person who is confident that God walks with them.

6 However, suppose the watchman sees the sword coming but doesn't blow the ram's horn, so that the people aren't warned, and the sword comes and takes away their lives. Then they have been taken away because of their iniquity, but I will hold the watchman accountable for their blood.' Ezekiel 33:6 (CSB).

CWASCs are typically Night Guard Churches. It is difficult being a Night Guard on a moonless night. However, with the help of the moon, that reflected light, the gentler light of experience and age, then it is a worthy and responsible job. It is necessary that somebody guards the community at its most vulnerable - whilst it sleeps. The Night Guard has a duty to continually survey the surrounding countryside, something they can only do if they stay awake and, when they see danger, to sound the alarm. Scripture seems to suggest that they are the antithesis of Cain – they are their brother's keeper. Any lack of sight, watchfulness and voice on their part is dangerous. It is a privilege to be a Night Guard, but one for whom failure carries a high price.

May I ask, 'Have the CWASC been shouting out the alarm to the national church, and if they have, what are they saying, and have we listened to them?'

And what of God? What does God do in the night, in the moonlight, with those churches that are called to such a ministry? The frailty and age of congregations, even their lack of numbers, is not an encumbrance or a brake to what God is capable of or what they can do.

Our garden is surrounded on two sides by high trees, thus creating lots of truly shady environments. It is no good bedding sun-loving plants in these areas as they do not thrive, obviously. It requires a search of a garden centre to find suitable ones. And to be frank, they are generally not as attractive as the hot sun variety. They are smaller, hardier and less frivolous. If they produce crops their harvest is limited. According to their nature they grow slowly, but boy do they hang in there.

I have known a few Night Guards as well. They are generally hardy too, not easily frightened, level headed and calm, content with their own company. God is the same in the night and in the day, yet in respect of his human charges he dials down the wattage. Having said that, you only need to read the psalms to see how active God's Spirit is during the long nights, when we are in bed and he acts out his thoughts and words through dreams and visions, and meets his faithful people in their watchings.

Night Guards are not just watching for evil, but good too. God watches in the night to observe our hearts and to respond to them. God tenderly waits for every little positive thought from us, whenever it comes. The CWASC is called to live with its limits and to love itself as God does.

[1] Unless the LORD builds a house, its builders labor over it in vain; unless the LORD watches over a city, the watchman stays alert in vain. Psalms 127:1 (CSB).

Even at night God is at work and night time work will be as successful, if the Lord is involved, as would daytime work.

God undergirds everything. He desires to be involved in every age and every stage of church life. We are called to accept this humbly. God's presence can be as much of a challenge and admonishment as an encouragement.

[2]"Stand in the gate of the house of the LORD and there call out this word: 'Hear the word of the LORD, all you people of Judah who enter through these gates to worship the LORD.
[3] "'This is what the LORD of Armies, the God of Israel, says: Correct your ways and your actions, and I will allow you to live in this place. [4] Do not trust deceitful words, chanting, "This is the temple of the LORD, the temple of the LORD, the temple of the LORD." [5] Instead, if you really correct your ways and your actions, if you act justly toward one another, [6] if you no longer oppress the resident alien, the fatherless, and the widow and no longer shed innocent blood in this place or follow other gods, bringing harm on yourselves, [7] I will allow you to live in this place, the land I gave to your ancestors long ago and forever. Jeremiah 7:2-7 (CSB).

CHAPTER 12 – Introvert V Extrovert In Personality and Unity WITH Evangelism In Action.

[2] I will indeed gather all of you, Jacob; I will collect the Remnant of Israel.
I will bring them together like sheep in a pen, like a flock in the middle of its fold. It will be noisy with people.
Micah 2:12 (CSB).

I once asked my Lay Reader whether she thought our church was introverted or extroverted. She agreed with me that we seem to have a greater number than average of introverts. I am an introvert – please do not believe that this is incompatible with a public ministry, I hasten to add. At times, I simply put on my public face, which I have learnt to adopt, and off I go. Probably, most people, because of that adopted demeanour, see me as an extrovert.

However, an introvert is somebody who resources themselves on their own, in quiet and splendid isolation. That is me. An extrovert resources themselves by heading for the nearest group of people. Cleary, I made the church in my own image! I know that sounds arrogant, but it is not. I am simply being pragmatic: the person I am, informed the way I led the church and was therefore attractive to those like myself. Is it a bad thing that the personality of a minister is one factor in the composition of a church, or a wonderful endorsement of the humanity of the ministry?

I also asked my Lay Reader whether she thought the present congregation – just below the average size numerically for a church congregation – would continue to attend if we were able to fulfil our often spoken of dreams and prayers by becoming a CWALC. She felt that most of them would feel uncomfortable in a CWALC and leave as it inevitably became much louder and busier.

How much human choice does God allow in fashioning our churches? I am ashamed to say, but confess with confidence, that I cannot be the only one to wonder on occasions how such and such a person got to be ordained: many other ministers are so 'other' to me and their ministries are, as a consequence, radically different from mine.

So, what is the answer? Well, you only need to look at the different people God chooses in Scripture to carry out his work. From the shy Moses, the homebird Jacob, to the grossly extrovert Solomon; to John the beloved disciple compared to Peter who could not keep his mouth or personality shut.

Churches are unlikely to be the same ever due to the differences in a whole range of factors, not simply the personality of the clergy, but social - economic factors as well. It is dangerous to think we should squash them all into the same shape. And this will inevitably mean that there will be differences in church style and temperament of worship. The time has come to be less critical of other's choices or other's discernments because the results are more nature than nurture.

The main factor that attracted me to offer myself for ministry in the Church of England was the wide spectrum of character, church style and practice [this now includes gender and one day fully, I hope, sexuality] into which I was convinced I would find a place and fit. In fact, after first my ACCM, my then bishop said he had realised that he had taken my quiet personality as lack of strength – implying he had been sparing in his support - but he now realised how steely I was. Too late for that one. I got through the next. It seems that God does allow for these differences and without chaffing as much about them as we do. Often is it our own lack of acceptance of other styles of ministry and the accompanying arrogance that causes the problems, as we judge others unworthy, judgements that God has no such thoughts about.

Over the years I have read several books written by former minsters of recognised big ministries in CWALCs who, under their tutelage, brought a particular church to life, and have now written a 'how to' guide on replicating such success. Indeed, attracted to some of the statements, I have tried such things myself over the years, though with no or very limited success. This I realise was not my failure to adopt the principles sufficiently well, but that this is not what God wanted for my situation. If God had wanted homogeneity, he would have only made one sort of flower in the world. Nature is our tutor as to how God embraces difference.

I cannot think of a reason any church should be labelled a failure, whatever its congregational size, if it is operating at an appropriate spiritual level within itself, its limits and gifts. Any judgment of a church must be much more subtle than purely economic or mathematical.

We need some way to measure the growth of a church historically and by personality as well as spirituality.

Why do those within the church judge other churches more harshly than as individuals they judge their neighbours. Is it to do with expectation? Do we judge churches more harshly because we forget they are made up of people just like ourselves?

[1] **LORD, who can dwell in your tent? Who can live on your holy mountain? [2] The one who lives blamelessly, practices righteousness, and acknowledges the truth in his heart— [3] who does not slander with his tongue, who does not harm his friend or discredit his neighbor, [4] who despises the one rejected by the LORD but honors those who fear the LORD, who keeps his word whatever the cost,** Psalms 15:1-4 (CSB).

[10] **Love one another deeply as brothers and sisters. Take the lead in honoring one another. [11] Do not lack diligence in zeal; be fervent in the Spirit; serve the Lord. [12] Rejoice in hope; be patient in affliction; be persistent in prayer. [13] Share with the saints in their needs; pursue hospitality. [16] Live in harmony with one another. Do not be proud; instead, associate with the humble. Do not be wise in your own estimation. [18] If possible, as far as it depends on you, live at peace with everyone.** Romans 12:10-13, 16, 18 (CSB).

Do not give a stone for bread! God does not call those on whom he lavishes his love unworthy. God made us as we are. Did you know that people become more introverted as they grow older? Psychologists call this intrinsic maturation.

Did you know that the CWASCs are like the widows of the church?

[22] **"You must not mistreat any widow or fatherless child.** Exodus 22:22 (CSB).

[18] **He executes justice for the fatherless and the widow, and loves the resident alien, giving him food and clothing**. Deuteronomy 10:18 (CSB)

[43] **Summoning his disciples, he said to them, "Truly I tell you, this poor widow has put more into the treasury than all the others.** Mark 12:43 (CSB).

A CWASC bears a resemblance to a monastic community for the married, old and disabled. What does it produce beyond caring for its members? A cooperative perhaps. If other churches will not make quiet spaces and appropriate freedoms for introverts will not God make up the lack? Why is a CWASC such a reproach to a successful church? Why can't they leave it alone? It is impossible to change an introvert.

Where can we find scriptural support for the necessity for churches of all sizes, church style and denominations to see a common purpose in lovingly working together? These words for Ezekiel give us a hint of the thinking of God as he observes the brokenness of his chosen people and their split into two dissimilar sized factions.

[5] **The word of the LORD came to me:** [16] **"Son of man, take a single stick and write on it: Belonging to Judah and the Israelites associated with him. Then take another stick and write on it: Belonging to Joseph—the stick of Ephraim—and all the house of Israel associated with him.** [17] **Then join them together into a single stick so that they become one in your hand.** Ezekiel 37:15-17 (CSB).

I would like to draw your attention to something Jesus

said:

[34] "I give you a new command: Love one another. Just as I have loved you, you are also to love one another. [35] By this everyone will know that you are my disciples, if you love one another." John 13:34-35 (CSB).

If it is true that God wants to combine the CWASC and the CWALC like two sticks in his hand with a common purpose and unity, it gives us an opportunity to look at evangelism in a new way. Clearly evangelism is part of the business of the church and we do try and do this in our social work and presentations of the gospel.

What it is saying in these two short verses is that in our visible unity we show people our discipleship. Here is what we should consider. Is it possible our failures in evangelism are more down to our lack of unity than our lack of effort? Like it or not we often excuse our disunity with our zeal. The Church of England has different factions within it. We call them church style and each one insists they are right.

Sadly, the very thing we long for has been spoilt by our own disharmony and not by any lack of prayer or commitment to our chosen form of evangelism. Perhaps we have got something wrong? We do not see these disagreements, debates, discussion, different theological interpretation, or liturgical priorities as anything more than that. Nevertheless, what they are is disunity. Jesus is telling us that the world will know we are disciples when we search out our disunity, name it and proceed together in unity. This will be enormously painful because it will involve acknowledging that we will never be the true church of God until we accept that we may not be right.

We will need to forego our own self-righteousness and humbly put others before ourselves, even those who worship or act differently to us.

Perhaps the reason the Church does not grow is because we do not pursue being one church together. Is it right to say that evangelism fails, not because the right words are not being used, but for the reason that all churches flout God's rule about being together? These verses tell us that it is by unity that we show we are disciples. This is the real impediment. Our visible discipleship is one of the greatest evangelistic tools we have. Why not use it?

I am suggesting that if we could find a new unity it would unleash a mighty work of the Holy Spirit across our land and bring with conviction a huge host of new believers into the kingdom and our churches. Why should it happen this way in particular, than what we have tried already? Well, because at the root it is based on obedience to Jesus. The instruction Jesus gives to us to love one another is a commandment and we disobey it at our peril. Finding unity will be the greatest challenge we face for we will need to stop insisting that our way is right and go as far as protecting the views of those with whom we disagree.

CHAPTER 13 – God Tests Churches.

[14] **As for the seed that fell among thorns, these are the ones who, when they have heard, go on their way and are choked with worries, riches, and pleasures of life, and produce no mature fruit.** Luke 8:14 (CSB).

do not harden your hearts as in the rebellion, on the day of testing in the wilderness, [9] where your ancestors tested me, tried me, and saw my works... Hebrews 3:8-9 (CSB).

[3] **because you know that the testing of your faith produces endurance.** James 1:3 (CSB).

I think it would be wrong to think that God allows unchecked enthusiasm. I recently heard Jesus described as a 'mover'.

'Move it! Move it!' the speaker said. It is a quote from a pop song. God and Jesus can be overpromoted as somebody who is always trying to do new things. If that is the case, what happens to the old things? Does it mean they weren't worthwhile or that God got bored with them? And what of continuity? If an act of service is worth doing once, it is worth doing several times and committing to. To leave it behind, to do a new thing – they are always exhilarating at first - leaves those who have come to rely on it in the lurch. As exciting as such passion is, and the sense it gives of palpable progress, it has more to do with a new slick advertising campaign than the church. It has become an insult to describe a church as steady, but infinitely better than giddy. The Bible tells us that a good steward brings both old and new out of his storeroom. Of course, it would be as wrong to side line the new and constantly bring out the stale stuff. Balance is appropriate.

This sense of perpetual change also gives little time for lessons to be learnt, long term lessons in particular. And it also presupposes that we somehow have God in our power as a sort of champing horse that we need hold back for fear he rushes on too fast.

The OT gives us several choice lessons about what God feels about sacrifice and how on occasions it bores and irritates him, especially when the acts of sacrifice do not mirror the heart that gives them. God would rather have something deeper from us.

I believe, more often than not, God acts as a parent and teacher rather than a cheerleader. He has a habit of uncalled for interventions and throwing up obstacles to our progress to test our mettle. He does this to bring about a greater sense of self-knowledge, God knowledge and trust from us.

It would be wrong to claim that these blockages, these hesitations to our ambition are, as some are wanting to claim, because Satan is particularly active in opposition to the church's progress and, consequently, we need to pray harder to battle through. Surely, at some deep level, it is a blasphemy against the Holy Spirit to call God's normal directive, involved relationship and actions in our lives, and that of our church, as a work of the devil. Simply because things are not going our way does not mean we are being opposed by the whole of the devil's kingdom. It might be our own pride or the possibility that we have plainly got ahead of ourselves, and we have come to believe that what we want is what God wants. If we call an action of God's, an action of Satan's: badly done everyone, badly done.

The way God talks of the church as his body gives us the strong hint that we may use examples of God's treatment of individuals, individual bodies even, as found in the Scripture, as a metaphor of how he might treat a church.

I do not want anyone to take away the idea that I am against evangelism. I have made it clear how important it is to share the Gospel. Rather, I am advocating that there is a parallel between the way God takes a deep interest in the soul of a new convert and begins his work within them, and the way he labours within their new church fellowship. None of the individuals in a church should expect to be spared from his exertions to produce from them, as living bricks, a corporate expression of what it is to be a Christian: as an individual body, so the body of the church. This will mean that God will allow impediments and provide complications consciously for this specific work, a work quite different from that which he pursues individually in us.

We live in a fallen world. The church lives in a fallen world. It shows its mettle not by its success, but by its perseverance. Those who conquer will get the rewards, we are told in Revelation; those in the end will be victorious. That, necessarily and historically, must include the possibility of many individual battles and skirmishes, lots of times when the war was in the balance, where we, or our churches, were hard pressed and where no human success was visible until God stepped in and we made it by the skin of our teeth.

Triumphalism has no place in the Christian faith and neither should it have a place in the vocabulary of the church. When things are going well - then is the time to tremble. Not because we fear God will fail us, but that perhaps another time of testing and trial is on its way – for our good. In our success we are called to deeper humility.

Think about how many of the psalms and prophets remind their hearers about the past. Remember the Exodus we are told, repeatedly. 'Times have been hard since, but remember how God rescued the people of faith in an exodus.' I recognise how this gives us a good blueprint for the Christian life. I think we sometimes read the Bible with too selective a view and do not see it as a whole. I am guilty of this myself. Particularly in the NT, it is easy to highlight in your own mind the times when there was a success, yet if you scrutinise the text more thoroughly you read of the problems too. For example, we read of Paul telling off the Corinthians for the sexual sin they had not dealt with without really engaging our imagination as to what that must have felt like. We use our imagination more readily to think of the good things.

Let me explain further. I have been on guided retreats where the leader has led us in an imaginative contemplation of Jesus feeding the 5000 and encouraged us, with our eyes shut, to be there. I have not once had such an experience of a guided retreat imagining the receipt of such a letter from Paul and being encouraged to give my imagination the opportunity to dwell on the effects of this held against my own unrepented sin in church. Just imagine if the old vicar's son, who still lives in the parish after his father died, begins a sexual relationship with his step mum whilst still attending church. It is an interregnum of course, so nobody feels able to do anything about it. A letter has been sent to the Archdeacon, but is off sick herself. Then the backbiting between those of a more romantic nature who want to give love a chance and the harsh, bitter evangelicals who say they will both roast in hell. Thus, the church comes to a car crash where all thoughts of anything else go out of the window. The old vicar's mentor writes an open letter to the church from abroad having heard of the situation. Powerful stuff. And what about Peter and Paul falling out. The church of the NT is real one. In among the deeply spiritual and miraculous stuff there is bad stuff happening.

Why should we expect it to be any different today?

The church is not a charmed community, but a deeply relevant one, warts and all, plus the Holy Spirit working in his inimical way.

May I reemphasise: if a church is a body, then surely it will live through the seven ages of man too. It will have a neonatal stage and an old age, with every stage of human physical, emotional and mental development in between. For churches to try and stay very young is a mistake. And to euthanise is a horrible wrong. Any attempt at eugenics will trouble God.

A further image that is found in Scripture, that relates to spiritual growth, is of a tree and its need for water. The tree growing by Ezekiel's River provides leaves for the healing of the nations. Little green shoots illustrate a church in its spring. A fig tree, cursed by Jesus, a church that is being given a last chance. Then there are vines, olive trees and the great oaks of Lebanon.

And of course, Jerusalem, the city that Jesus wept over and for whom there are so many prophecies; where finally all the churches, whether a CWASC or a CWALC, will be gathered.

The historical perspective of salvation history of Israel also speaks strongly to the fluctuations that the Church should expect and embrace in its corporate life together.

So how should a church respond to God's periods of testing?

For the LORD your God is testing you to know whether you love the LORD your God with all your heart and all your soul. Deuteronomy 13:3b (CSB).

It should rejoice that God thinks it worthy, displaying humility in success and trustfulness in failure and catastrophe. God's work embraces both the welcome of new souls and the development of his children. God values churches not simply as evangelism tools, but with a personal interest to make them as holy as possible in all the relationships between the faithful, quite apart from their usefulness.

CHAPTER 14 - When God Closes A Church.

[9] **I will put this third through the fire; I will refine them as silver is refined and test them as gold is tested. They will call on my name, and I will answer them. I will say, 'They are my people,' and they will say, 'The LORD is our God.'"** Zechariah 13:9 (CSB).

It is time to consider what might be the reasons to close a church building and disperse the congregation to other ministries. However, it is right to ask whether the same criteria apply to divine and human agencies in this decision.

[32] **For I take no pleasure in anyone's death." This is the declaration of the Lord GOD. "So repent and live!** Ezek 18:32 (CSB).

The Master Chef series of television programmes on the BBC make enormously good television, yet are very painful to watch. It is clear that all of the contestants try their hardest. Eventually, the decisive moment comes and they must present their finished dishes to be tried and judged by the judges. You can see in the faces that they are trying not to be disappointed. According to their own lights they did their best. In fact, they would have not even got into the competition if they had not had some confidence and self-belief. Nevertheless, you can see how the judgments can be like hammer blows, causing some to well up in tears at the result.

Then all the churches will know that I am the One who examines minds and hearts, and I will give to each of you according to your works. Revelation 2:23 (CSB).

At the end of the day, it does not really matter how well we think we have done nor do our judgments of our fellow competitor's matter. It is the judge's summation that matters most. The series of seven letters to the churches in the Book of Revelation make painful reading. The Book of Revelation shows us that the essence of a church is represented by its presiding spirit [angel]. It matters little whether they are real churches or not. What they reveal, as we will see in more detail later in the chapter, is the kind of things God is looking for in a church, both what pleases him and what does not, and how a church may partially please him, yet still fall short in some details. They show how negative influences can continue long after they should have been dealt with and, finally, the wonderful consequences that lie ahead for those who conquer.

It is right and appropriate that we use these judgments as a check list to measure the progress of our own churches. And although they seem harsh it does not appear that a CWASC needs to quail at their directness any more than a CWALC. In fact, there is no mention of size or finances at all in any of the churches cited.

I mentioned before how it would be good that when churches are assessed they are done so on factors beyond those two. Here is the basis of such a report on the spiritual health of a church. Imagine if the bishops went around their churches with a checklist, from this passage in Revelation, in their hand and then dared to hold it up against those they visit and then spoke to what they found. I can't imagine how that might happen without hurting. This is an upsetting list. Maybe we are too keen to ameliorate? The monastic communities dare to make such enquiries of their members and the brothers or sisters are commanded to submit. Even so these dissections are found helpful, if challenging, when done in the correct spirit.

Fortune favours the brave. If a church throws up its hands in horror at such a challenge, then maybe it is right that they close. All this feeds into the need for a great humility in those who are judged and those who judge.

Anyone with any self-awareness will know that they are constantly making such judgments in their minds all the time. Is there not a possibility that we can speak of such matters aloud?

There is so much at stake. Listen to this wonderful list of consequences, from the account in the Book of Revelation, for the churches and the individuals within them that conquer:

"Anyone who has an ear should listen to what the Spirit says to the churches. I will give the victor the right to eat from the tree of life, which is in God's paradise. Revelation 2:7 (CSB).

The victor will never be harmed by the second death. Revelation 2:11 (CSB).

I will give the victor some of the hidden manna. I will also give him a white stone, and on the stone a new name is inscribed that no one knows except the one who receives it. Revelation 2:17 (CSB).

The one who is victorious and keeps My works to the end: I will give him authority over the nations — [27] and he will shepherd them with an iron sceptre; he will shatter them like pottery — just as I have received this

from My Father. 28 I will also give him the morning star. Revelation 2:26-28 (CSB).

the victor will be dressed in white clothes, and I will never erase his name from the book of life but will acknowledge his name before My Father and before His angels. Revelation 3:5 (CSB).

The victor: I will make him a pillar in the sanctuary of My God, and he will never go out again. I will write on him the name of My God and the name of the city of My God — the new Jerusalem, which comes down out of heaven from My God — and My new name. Revelation 3:12 (CSB).

The victor: I will give him the right to sit with Me on My throne, just as I also won the victory and sat down with My Father on His throne. Revelation 3:21 (CSB).

Is this not a formidable list of positive consequences for those who are victorious?

So, let us start at the beginning. The descriptions of the churches are a mixed bag. I have had a debate with one of my colleagues trying to decide which one comes off best. We could not agree! I have gone for the church of Sardis, but only just though! They are as good as dead, their work is incomplete, **yet**, nevertheless, there are a few remaining in the congregation who are OK. Their presence seems to bring hope and protection to the rest, however moribund they appear. How relevant to the poor CWASC that I have typified in this book as numerically constrained, rural and urban, problematic churches, albeit hanging on in crumbling buildings. Look how things look so different from God's point of view, when you stop measuring by the world's standards. Nevertheless, all the critiques of the churches in the Book of Revelation are very painful to read. We find common themes keep coming up.

Firstly, notice how much good God has to say about them. If you gather all the praise from the seven churches, we get quite an impressive list, one which would please any church, whatever its congregational size.

God praises them for their labour, their general endurance, particularly against slander; their intolerance of evil; the way they test their leaders; their perseverance and their fortitude in suffering; that they do not succumb to weariness, but keep going despite affliction, poverty and imprisonment, even those who live near Satan's throne; their weakness even, which is not condemned, but sympathised with. You see they have kept God's word and not denied his name. Just imagine if we sent some secret shopper with this list to our local churches and see how many ticks they came back with.

Unfortunately, these positive qualities are degraded by the negative. One church is tolerating the Nicolaitans and another bad teaching. Imagine how that would play out if a church complained about its vicar, their poor teaching, and took it right up to the bishop. Yet if they do not, are they failing by denying their own need for sound teaching? Remember what we read in Nehemiah about the teaching ministry of Levites who accompanied Ezra!

7 Jeshua, Bani, Sherebiah, Jamin, Akkub, Shabbethai, Hodiah, Maaseiah, Kelita, Azariah, Jozabad, Hanan, and Pelaiah, who were Levites, explained the law to the people as they stood in their places. 8 They read out of

the book of the law of God, translating and giving the meaning so that the people could understand what was read. Nehemiah 8:7-8 (CSB).

Of course, the bad teaching mentioned here in the Book of Revelation is about idolatry and sexual matters, yet poor world views and unsound doctrine in preachers leads to untold harm and, at worst, cults. Underlying this is a lack of repentance. See how the good qualities can be washed away by the bad. How awful to have your church called lukewarm or moribund. It would be exceedingly painful to hear any of this. Yet, would it be of value especially if it had a positive effect? And who is daring enough to make such an enquiry? Who in the church has enough courage to give the truthful answers? It will require real humility and spiritual fitness to be the one who utters the hard word. This is the opposite of 'hushing things up' and more about admitting one's faults, confessing and repenting. Such radical assessment would be other worldly. The way of the world is not to admit failure. Nevertheless, if faith in God begins with some sort of repentance, should not the life of a church corporate be marked with such conversation?

And finally, what will the judgment be? Will God shut a church? Churches have shut; we see the vestiges of ruined walls scattered around the landscape. Henry the 8th, admittedly for personal reasons - greed and self-glorification - was a real dose of salts. The Book of Homilies marks a recognition of how bad teaching was and the need to restore it. God does not rejoice in death:

32 For I take no pleasure in anyone's death." This is the declaration of the Lord GOD. "So repent and live! Ezek 18:32 (CSB).

However, his patience is not inexhaustible and, despite my assertions that a CWASC may be viable in ways that do not register in the way we test churches by numbers and finance, there must come a point when a church community is such a negative witness that:

> [5] **Remember then how far you have fallen; repent, and do the works you did at first. Otherwise, I will come to you and remove your lampstand from its place, unless you repent.** Revelation 2:5 (CSB).

God will come and remove the lampstand or at else get his representatives on earth to do so.

That, however, is not the end. We need to ask, 'What then?' What if our local church shuts? What provision is to be made for those dispossessed and those whose responsibility it is. It is well known in Anglican circles that as a denomination we do not travel well. If you close all the churches in a Benefice for one Sunday to have a combined service in one of the churches you can guarantee you will only get half the congregation you would have done if all had remained open. Perhaps we have over-parented our congregations and, even when they should be mature, remain like bird chicks, who never having learned to feed themselves, are unable to leave their nests. Conceivably this is one cause of bad teaching by the church leadership: they are always tempted to keep within their congregations' comfort zones.

Largely, churches seem to shut because they have reached the end of the line with respect to finances. It used to be that the building would cost too much to repair; now it is often because they cannot afford a minister. If the end of a church is predicated by finances, because it is clear that a congregation can no longer afford a minister – a stipendiary clergyperson - then, if it were possible to remove this obstacle, would not otherwise viable churches be able to continue?

This will be addressed in a later chapter.

What then of the poor Christians who cannot afford, or are unable, due to age or disability, to relocated to a CWALC? Do they become members of the hidden seven thousand of Elijah? Would they not be like one of those fire bushes that only needs water to revive it? Or like poppies waiting for the soil to be disturbed to regenerate. I believe it is important that all churches, whatever their state, to be allowed to preserve their true dignity. Christianity is a religion that is foundationally hopeful. So, it is right to believe and hope that even after a physical building has gone, or a minister to provide a focus, faith lives on, albeit temporarily dormant. Can we read always read the closure of a church as a judgement? Is faith and church-going the same?

Certainly, all this would seem stark without God's love. Even though the closure may appear to be an entirely human decision it is impossible to say with confidence that we are motived solely by love or that our decision was pure. We can say that of God though. Is the closure of a church a judgment? Yes. It is not, however, the Final Judgment.

SECTION C – HOW IT SHINES SO BEAUTIFULLY.

CHAPTER 15 – The River Flows Slower At The Bank.

[20] So follow the way of good people, and keep to the paths of the righteous. [21] For the upright will inhabit the land, and those of integrity will remain in it; Proverbs 2:20-21 (CSB).

I believe there is only one acceptable conclusion: God establishes churches with small congregations on purpose. They are not an act of completed creation, rather a work in progress, for God is not absent, he also nurtures and is involved in the further organic development of his 'making'. Nor are the CWASC the dying remnants of a great empire. Simply because they may have appeared, by virtue of their size, to be prosperous once, does not mean that in their smaller manifestation they have begun to decay or displease God. They are simply one stage in the seven ages of a church. Like a human, they may progress from neonatal to geriatric. Everybody is attracted to youth, to bright fresh young churches, but each stage of life has a purpose. And as we experience - some of God's purposes are inscrutable! Metaphors abound to encourage us and confuse us, both in Scripture and in the world: those parts of our anatomy that seem more useful than others - liver versus appendix; the slag heaps of mines are now being reworked for the previously discarded, once worthless, now valued trace elements; the world provides safe harbours and docks for the ships of life to escape from storms and for embarkation, safety and repair; birds could roam freely in Solomon's Temple; sometimes God makes a CWALC into a CWASC as a strategic retreat in a changing society. Why does God do this? Because he can, he wills and he acts. God's sovereign will embraces all differences, and both small and large endeavours.

It may be that the CWASCs have been created like this, or allowed to remain by God as they are, or even diminished by him on purpose as a kind gift to the sort of people who are unlikely to find solace anywhere else. CWASCs are not failures; they are acts of serendipity. If in a local, geographical area, the need for a CWALC is fulfilled by the actual existence of a CWALC then it does not need to be greedy. Pride may lead it to think it can be everything to everyone or that its theology will fulfil all. This is not true - it can live in peace, secure in the knowledge that it is as much loved by God as its CWASC neighbour. CWALCs do not need to conclude that its local CWASCs need to be rescued or improved, and certainly not act on it. Leave the CWASC alone please. Some will create pejorative labels to make themselves feel better, even see them as an object of charity, but please do not feel a need to mend them without first sensitively asking those who worship there what they might want from their larger neighbour. Arrogance has no place in inter-church relationships.

God can give a space outside the camp, or up in the mountain, or in the wilderness where things survive without any proper facilities, for those who need to go outside to rest.

Rivers flow faster in the middle. If you throw two logs in a river, one in the middle and one near the bank. The one in the middle will soon disappear out of sight, whereas the one close to the bank will move quite slowly and is likely to get snagged repeatedly, even completely stuck for years, as it rots away in the water, until chance moves it again.

It is very difficult to remain stationary in the middle, in the fast-flowing water you find there. A boat would need to turn around and power forward constantly just to remain in one spot. Dropping an anchor is difficult if not impossible, as the water might be too deep. Most boats go to the bank, or send a tender to shore to communicate. If a small boat gets washed and dragged into the middle of the current it might be lost in the turbulence of the river or swamped by the wash of bigger boats.

The Bible tells us that a river went out from Eden to water the garden and this river then became four mighty rivers that irrigate the entire region. It seems to be saying there was a spring in Eden. If you have ever visited a natural spring it is puzzling how something so slow and weak can become so strong and fast miles away. Of course, it is joined by the run off from the land bordering the river.

Was the river that flowed from Eden as miraculous as the river that flowed from the temple in Ezekiel? That river grew supernaturally deeper and deeper very quickly. There cannot have been sufficient run off for it to happen naturally. It was a miracle: water seemed to be reproducing itself. This is not as unlikely as it appears, for the Holy Spirit is described as living water and when you let that image into your mind it will soon make many other connections if you know the Bible well. Rivers get many mentions in Scripture, yet it is on the banks that most things happen: where the water runs the slowest.

The interface of river and bank is fragile and vulnerable to turbulence. If the river ran fast here, the bank would be undercut, crumble and fall away – as occurs on bends. Who can forget oxbow lakes from geography lessons! What would happen if nature were reversed and the river ran fast all along the bank? It is all a bit counterintuitive, like the fact of the anomalous expansion of water that causes water to freeze from the top down, and so prevents all our oceans becoming frozen solid. As there is a wonderful, created, perfect harmony in nature, would not God also compose a perfect harmony in the church and its local expressions? How negligent of God if he exhausted himself making Nature then only to be too tired to do anything but a botched job on the Church. The Scripture seems to tell a different tale: that he spent more time and effort on the church and that it is human beings who tend to spoil it.

Oh, dear what can the matter be? Slow churches versus fast churches, loud churches versus quiet churches and hot churches versus cold churches?

Perhaps we do not really understand God or spend enough time trying to find out. Perhaps God makes things as they are to reflect his unknown purposes. God makes/allowed CWASCs on purpose. And try as we might we can never gainsay that. Maybe being a CWASC is a higher calling rather than a lower one? Being in a CWASC can be difficult in the extreme, but does not God reward people by given them hard things to do? God is particular about things. My own church became a CWASC, as many did, because of the accelerating secularisation of society. However, when it had lost its fat – those for whom the church was no more than a special interest group - and all that were left were the ones with a genuine faith, even if they were reticent or too shy to speak about it, then, when it had become truly a CWASC it was a happy church with a good atmosphere; and over the years we accumulated a few Christians from other churches that liked our way of doing things and we saw a few conversions and much deepening of faith. And so, we might have continued if the scrutiny of judgment and trial by the ordeal of money and numbers had not brought it to an end. The problem of money does need to be resolved if CWASCs are to be allowed to thrive in their own way. [More of this later.]

One of my personal struggles has been at what point to begin to call myself an author, writer or novelist. In my heart I believed I was, but fell afoul of the standards of the world that seemed to say I was only really an author if I won the Booker Prize. I have sold a few of my books over the years and given a good number away. However, it has been writing this book that has helped me most because I can see now that I am 'a novelist, with a small number of readers', NWASNOR, and I should not deny myself that title simply because I am not a novelist with a huge number of readers [NWALNOR]. I find myself in a lot of company. It has become a matter of confidence and self-worth and this also is how a CWASC validates itself. Pejorative names are corrosive.

So, what! We are moored at the bank, we have not enough crew to set off into the deep water, we might be stuck here forever unless God changes something for us. Let us not give up hope though. Our confidence is in the fact that God calls us a church and not how others perceive us.

Of course, there are other places the water runs slowly, one is at the bottom of the main current – sunk. We do not want to go there. And neither do we want to attempt to moor on the outside of a bend!

The bank is good; trees grow there, the ones that draw water from the river and provide the food for the nations. God offers Living Water to the most broken of people and congregations. On any day you choose to pick, it can be good to be a CWASC. What a high calling from God!

CHAPTER 16 - The Beauty Of The Last Stretch.

[12] **Afterwards, Samuel took a stone and set it upright between Mizpah and Shen. He named it Ebenezer, explaining, "The Lord has helped us to this point."** 1 Sam 7:12 (CSB).

[7] **But as for you, be strong; do not be discouraged, for your work has a reward."** 2 Chron 15:7 (HCSB)

There are lots of 'end of chapter' moments in the Bible: the expulsion of Adam and Eve from Eden; the death of Abel; the destruction of the Tower of Babel; the flooding of the earth; Abram leaving his home; the Exodus; the destruction of Solomon's Temple by the Babylonians; the destruction of the Temple, following the earthly life of Jesus, by the Romans; the Diaspora of the early church. Some have good consequences immediately, some do not; some have good outcomes ultimately, some do not; some seem to have no significance at all. A few have a new beginning immediately, others eventually: like the people of Israel reaching their Promised Land and the Babylonian Jews being allowed to return and rebuild Jerusalem.

There is a lot of patience and waiting involved, a lot of testing and growth and none of it is a smooth straight line. We must know in our lives, if we have been Christians for some time, that our own personal salvation history is littered with initially unrecognised wrong turnings, bypasses and retracing our steps. Nevertheless, there is something very beautiful about the final stretch.

As we read the Gospels, we come eventually to that sense that Jesus has turned his footsteps for the last time to Jerusalem. I have explained to numbers of baptism preparation classes for parents how the Gospels give increasing attention to the last week of Jesus life, because, to the writers, that was the most important part of the narrative, especially the resurrection. The beauty comes in the wonderful way that God's purposes, which at time seem to wallow indecisively, all come together in one glorious wholeness.

I hope you have a sense in your own life, as you pass from one stage to another, that you gave it your best shot. It is something to aim for. I retain a quiet satisfaction on leaving my last parish, where I was for 26 years, that my achievements might never be measured by the prevailing ways of judging churches in my day, but that my offering of time, talent and energy was acceptable. And that at the Judgment, I will not answer for how others responded to my ministry, rather, how I fulfilled my calling to God. What a relief.

Other people's last stretches, as recounted in the Scriptures do not end so well. The People of Israel only got into the Promised Land when the naysayers were allowed to die out. In addition, they never completed the job of driving out the other tribes. David messed up and ended his life in a tense moment when his chosen heir Solomon nearly missed becoming king in his place. Solomon himself went off piste by the end of his life, led astray by his foreign wives.

Of course, some of the Biblical Last Stretches seem disproportionally long. A few years ago, I attended a secular conference on death. The conclusion: people are living longer, but not necessarily in good health. They suffer for longer! To the people involved the last stretch feels eternally overextended by God: waiting for Isaac to be born; four hundred years in Egypt until the Exodus; forty years in the wilderness; the last years of David's life; the seventy years of exile until a generation almost disappears. Waiting for the Fat Lady to sing is more bearable! With only death ahead of that.

How are we to arrange our lives so we have a good death? Impelled by the sense of Jesus' return, we need to keep going, not to get somewhere or achieve something, more money or numbers, but because we wait, busy.

'O lord, let me not live to be useless,' prayed John Wesley.

A good life, a good final stretch is about being and not doing. The endings in Scripture are an extended metaphor for us to lay on top of our understanding on what it means to be a church. Each church has its own personality and its own calling.

First, we must find our way through the conundrum of the Universal Church being the sum of individual churches and, that both the universal and the individual, are in themselves the body of Christ.

Each church must find its own way. How it will happen? I am not sure – they must answer for themselves. The ministers will answer for their ministry in some way, yet how individual members answer for their own behaviour in church remains to be seen. How often are good initiatives and good things to do torpedoed by some obfuscating and often emotionally damaged person? Church councils and positions of authority in the church seem to act as magnets to the unstable at times. I am not talking about normal differences of opinion, but more evil intent. Those who are objectionable for the sake of it. This is one strength of a CWALC - it is easier for them to side-line somebody without the necessity for a confrontation. Such confrontations are part of the CWASC's ministry and are necessary if the church is to dance to God's tune and not theirs, whatever the consequences. I will not be the only one to end up in the national press for such a challenge.

As members of the Church Universal, we all live under the sentence of the End Times. End times that have been going on for two millennia and with no sense, except for a few panics over natural phenomena during history, that the end might come tomorrow.

After a great battle at Mizpah between the Israelites and the Philistines we read

12 **Afterwards, Samuel took a stone and set it upright between Mizpah and Shen. He named it Ebenezer, explaining, "The LORD has helped us to this point."** 1 Sam 7:12 (CSB)

Ebenezer means 'stone for help'.

Whether we really are in the last day of the universe and God's judgment is speeding towards us in the next week; or whether we are at the beginning of our church taking off and would feel cheated if God actually came; or our church appears to be limping towards the final collapse of the building because we can no longer afford to repair it; or the last active member of the congregation's funeral is today and we realise an uncomfortable future lies ahead, each one of us can say , **"The LORD has helped us to this point."**

When I was a child, we travelled north for my grandmother's funeral and we stayed in her house as preparations were finalised. I became friendly with a local lad my own age and he showed me the primitive weapon he had made. I have no idea what it was called, but it worked a little like a sling shot. It was a garden cane with feathers at one end like an arrow, and a heavy lump of metal at the other. You did not launch it by throwing it as you would a spear, but by tying a string at the end with a slip knot so it would release as the machine took flight. It meant that as you threw it, it was not only impelled by the strength of your arm, but also by the force of the slingshot of the string. This gave it an extra heft. It was wonderful, and goodness knows what would have happened if it had hit anybody. In other words, it was pushed from behind. Churches with well documented histories can be encouraged when they read of these events to understand how their present-day actions are being forced forward from behind in the achievements of previous generations.

The first incumbent of my church began in 1301. His ministry carried it forward into the new century. Successive ministries pushed it forward further, my own hopefully included. This Is something that younger church plants, with no history, do not have. Their push from behind has been replaced by the power of the reach of their sending church.

In all cases: **"The Lord has helped us to this point."** 1 Sam 7:12b (CSB).

We cannot see the future, but we can take note of the past. How much of the Bible is about remembrance? Being urged to remember what God did is a frequent meme. The last stretch becomes bearable by the recollection of being fed and strengthened by God's engagement in the past. It happens in our own lives too does not it. After waiting for ten long years for my call to ordained ministry to be fulfilled and all the attendant pain of seeing others preferred before me, and that haunting sense of failure and loss that I might never make it, I found eventually that this extended wait has stood me in good stead over the years. I am more patient when the things I sense what God wants from me are delayed.

Of course, there is encouragement for the future too. All the many prophecies hover as prospective titbits as well as the wonderful confectionary of exquisite delights from the Book of Revelation.

It is helpful to hear the Bible tell us that the natural life span of a human is 70 years or 80 if you're lucky. We can see a certain rhythm in that and can make some plans when we are entering the last stretch of our life and need to make plans for a good death. What of the life span of a church though? My own church, and there was probably one before it on the same site, has the prospective lifespan of a Methuselah.

What I am attempting is to flag up the incomprehensible inability on our own part, maybe arrogance rather than ignorance, to take what we see in our own human lives, and in the impermanence of nature, and then not take this as a metaphor we should apply to our church. The exodus to heaven will see us leave our buildings behind. We might get a spiritual body, but I am not expecting heaven to be populated by Norman churches or modern behemoths. Churches will cease to exist; we will live in a city. There is not even to be a temple. The necessity of heaven will sweep away a lot of what we presently hold dear. We have become too precious about the geography and the physicality of our church buildings. We have allowed a sentimentality to overtake us. When I speak of a CWASC, I am not talking of a small building, necessarily constrained, to have a numerically small congregation. I am talking about the local expression for church - people only. People who could very easily meet in a house, as the early church did, or outside, as the persecuted church does. Stipendiary clergy have one advantage over the people who retire from secular work: we lose our job, our house and our church building all in one go. It is challenging and upsetting, but also very liberating. When we begin to pack up our vicarages, we find how much we have accumulated and see how small our new house is. What a wonderful relief to be forced to get rid of a lot of it. At the very least we need to move out of the parish and find another church building to meet Christians in.

For my own part it was a delight to go to other churches and be ministered to for a good six months before settling to one. It made me realise I had been living in an ecclesiastical bubble. My church suited me and I did not always notice the changes happening beyond it. It is important that we all take forays into the world beyond our own church walls to get the news, good or bad, of what is going on.

If you have not noticed: the church in England is plagued by the upkeep of an enormous number of irrelevant buildings. This is not the same argument as speaking up for the CWASCs. Our over sentimentality about buildings is a curse. Let us face it, is it not ridiculous that a benefice with 15 congregations in 15 building only totals the same congregational numbers as a CWALC, yet hampers its minister by insisting that he services them all in their own building? It is crazy, surely? A situation like that is not the Beauty of the Last Stretch. It may be the selfishness or the ugliness of the Last Stretch. The CofE is facing a financial crisis where it can no longer support such a large number of stipendiary clergy. That fact alone probably heralds the beginning of the Last Stretch. We need to find the beauty in that reality. The CWASCs I am defending in this book are so named because there are few visible Christians in the area it serves able to gather together. I am not in the business of defending the indefensible: it is not the same as several CWASCs, in a reasonably sized geographical area who, apart from pride and a misplaced loyalty to a building, might become one fellowship there. CWASCs have a definite place in the repertoire of the church and I have written this book because of my love of them and a desire for them to thrive for all the right reasons. However, I do not condone selfishness.

<u>CHAPTER 17 - The Sum Of The Parts</u>.

[1] **See what great love the Father has given us that we should be called God's children—and we are! The reason the world does not know us is that it did not know him.** 1 John 3:1 (CSB).

[1] **Therefore, there is now no condemnation for those in Christ Jesus,** Romans 8:1 (CSB).

[9] **You, however, are not in the flesh, but in the Spirit, if indeed the Spirit of God lives in you. If anyone does not have the Spirit of Christ, he does not belong to him.** Romans 8:9 (CSB).

Oh, go on I'll admit it - I am 69. Apart from a few teeth I have not lost anything yet. I have had a few repairs and some of the parts do not work as well, particularly my eyes and ears. I am still the sum of my parts though. We won't go there today, but I am surprised how many parts of us we can lose and still function.

As a child I enjoyed making Airfix kits. As I got better, I not only glued them together, but painted them too. The more effort I put into them the prouder I became. You can imagine my horror then, after many hours constructing a WWII aeroplane and carrying it carefully up to my bedroom for display, that, as I withdrew my hand, the sleeve of my jumper caught one of the propellers and dragged it involuntarily onto the floor. I do not remember if I cried, but I should have done.

A couple of years ago I spied in a shop a plastic kit for a car engine. As a keen mechanic I bought it. And it was magic! When I put it together it ran, with the help of a battery box, like a real engine. There were sound effects that reproduced the turning of the ignition, the whine of the starter motor and the first ignition. Wonderful. God constructed the world out of various parts the book of Genesis tells us.

Of course, I have not quoted the entire saying, for as my chapter heading alludes to: the whole is greater than the sum of the parts. In the box of my engine kit was a sheet of paper that listed the parts I should find there. I was able to check they were all there before I began. The Bible also contains lists of the parts of various things. I have already mentioned creation. The final, most important part of that, was humankind. It would not have 'run' otherwise. Salvation history would not work without the final part of the assemblage: the Messiah. In addition, we find other lists in Scripture: the twelves tribes of Israel; the three parts of God – Father, Son and Holy Spirit; the Passover meal with its details for the various food stuffs to gather; the first Eucharist and its bread and wine. We even find wonderful stuff for the anoraks among us: how to build the Ark and construct the Tabernacle; the seven words on the cross; the various lists of horses in the book of Revelation; even the seven groups of seven years that make the jubilee. Each whole being greater than the sum of the parts. The NT speaks of the body and its functions, emphasising that hands need feet and so on. And of course, the Church Universal is a list of all the churches that make its total. I am going to let God decide which ones to include!

If, however, we were to compare the sum of the parts of a CWASC to other churches, what conclusion would we come to? Firstly, the list for the CWASC is much shorter.

There seems to be some conspicuous absences – an organist, a children's worker and a teacher. Paul tells us he has become accustomed to want and surfeit, and manages both well. As he travelled around, he must have planted and visited churches that in his day would be a CWASC or a CWALC, yet not once does he give any clue about this. They are always the church of ... a place name; neither was he burdened by saints' names. My last church was St. Michael the Archangel, which I always romantically thought gave it a quaint flavour of church committed to spiritual warfare, so fitting as it stood on the edge of the town in which I lived, on a bluff over the railway line, a visible guardian for those who came by train. As I said, I am a romantic!

There had been a Methodist church in the parish once and there was an independent chapel of indeterminate affiliation about a mile from the church. The next nearest Anglican church was three miles away. No distance at all with a car but, as we all know, geography is everything.

Even now my church has become part of a larger benefice it retains its own identity. Having been on its own - I only had one building - it is now one part of a larger sum of parts in a group of three. What has changed though is the loss of its own minister for the moment, who hopefully will be restored. Like it as we may the presence of a minister does seem to be one of the indispensable parts of a church. My model engine would not work without the battery pack. This is not to bring greater honour to one part – it would be against Paul's wishes. As I said at the beginning, although it is amazing how life may continue even when a great number of body parts are missing, it cannot go on without a liver for instance. There are certain parts that are necessary to a church to vivify it. The liver, like a minister, is only a servant and often does no more than purify the bad blood in the body!

There are other necessary parts, but without soul and spirit, without breath, nothing lives. Without any sense of the presence of Jesus or the Holy Spirit within a church community, even if they have the most splendid building in the world for clothes, it is a whitewashed tomb, a dead thing. It might expound wonderful, pharisaic teaching and practice, but without the Spirit it remains moribund.

What little attention the CWASC often pay to the most important factor in their survival. For distracted by the building, the money and the need to keep up numbers, they take their eyes of the ball. I was a maths teacher before I was ordained, I know all about sums and equations: they need a solution, an answer. Some are impossible to solve because a number has been missed out. The number three - the Trinity - is a good number for such occasions! Ha-ha.

1 See what great love the FATHER has given us that we should be called God's children—and we are! The reason the world does not know us is that it did not know him. 1 John 3:1 (CSB).

1 Therefore, there is now no condemnation for those in CHRIST JESUS, Romans 8:1 (CSB).

9 You, however, are not in the flesh, but in the SPIRIT, if indeed the Spirit of God lives in you. If anyone does not have the Spirit of Christ, he does not belong to him. Romans 8:9 (CSB).

CHAPTER 18 – The Best It Can Do.

[21] **Praise the LORD, all His armies, His servants who do His will**. Psalms 103:21 (CSB).

Although we relentlessly promote the church as a body, we fail to capitalise on the image by allowing ourselves to benefit from anthropomorphising it. When John the Divine writes to the seven churches at the beginning of the Book of Revelation he does not address them as part of the Church Universal or even a local expression of the Body of Christ, but rather he addresses the angel of the churches and then says, 'You…' It is personal.

Admittedly it is confusing for as we think of the church as the body and Christ as its head, we imply that the church on its own is a headless body. Sadly, this is how we are often perceived – running around as a headless chicken!

Often, we are denied the chance to express the unique personality of our church and show how it differs from others. I think it would be a very good exercise to ask our congregations to list the key features of the personalities of our churches; an objective exercise within an imaginative medium.

It would also reveal where the church is in its history. I encountered a real struggle in my late 60s to declare my true nature over a matter: I felt embarrassed to admit that my days of getting down on the floor to play with my grandchildren had probably ended. Not only do I have a hearing disability, which makes it difficult to hear them, but... well... it was uncomfortable for me to sit on the floor. This was beyond a sacrifice and was doing me no good physically. Sometimes we must own up to what is the best we can do. It may not always have been the best, and one day things might improve, but truth can only liberate us when we tell it. My church, in the years preceding my retirement, began to be more honest about itself. We acknowledged that the youth work was unlikely to return and were comforted when the diocese admitted that they now saw the new focus of youth work as being through schools, and church schools in particular. In addition, the archdeacon produced a very helpful demographic survey. This revealed the great number of retired people who lived in our parish and therefore helped us to reconsider where we were putting our energies. It gave us the opportunity to tell the truth about ourselves and to see that, consequently, our prime mission field, using our own reduced stamina, should be the newly retired.

As for man, his days are like grass — he blooms like a flower of the field;
16 **when the wind passes over it, it vanishes, and its place is no longer known.** Psalms 103:15-16 (CSB)

We fail to make the connection that because all life is temporal, so we should read the life of a church. That does not mean the church only surges forward at full throttle all the time and then stops dead, but rather that churches can diminish as part of a natural process. There will eternally be the Church, there may not always be our church.

We fail to strictly analyse what it is about a CWASC, our CWASC even, that makes it unique and how that impacts on its strengths and weaknesses.

In a CWASC everyone must participate. In my own church there was a very sad episode when the ruling clique of lay people, who had dominated the church for years, felt obliged, for various reasons, to support an individual who had compromised themselves and then felt unable to back down. The result was that several church officers left, leaving us with a much smaller congregation of individuals who had no experience of leadership. Far from being a disaster it was more like those forest situations that benefit from a lightning strike and inferno to cleanse the ground, allowing new growth to regenerate quickly. It was amazing. Several of the remnant took a large gulp and said they would give it a go. Two new churchwardens stepped forward and, without the benefit of the old hands to guide them, knuckled down and became excellent. In many other areas, however, we were faced with the bleak realisation that we fell short; we were facing challenge and possible failure. By God's grace we moved forward and, although we never recovered and became that larger numerical congregation again, there was a material change in the atmosphere of the church, which in time contributed to a small, but steady stream of people joining us. It did not sadly cover the natural wastage by death, so although we evolved, our numbers remained constant. How galling! We became a CWASC! However hard we tried, we knew that we would never be strong enough to prevail in some things, unless by a miracle of God. A miracle that we prayed for and hoped for, yet never saw. This is the stark reality for many churches behind the numbers game. Their congregations are faithful, godly people, but weak, old and diminished by time. They are involuntarily forced to display a view of themselves to the world which is not the whole truth and they feel humiliated by it.

I read recently a helpful explanation of the contrast between resignation and surrender. When we resign to something it makes us resentful because we have been forced to. If we surrender, bizarrely, we remain in charge because we accept God's will for that moment. Is it always God's will that every single church grows? I find nothing to support that assertion in Scripture, but I do find plenty to encourage us to surrender to God's will, even if it goes against our desires.

There were times I wanted to vocalise to our critics what our church felt, 'Sometimes, when we see you scrutinise our church, even if you do not speak of your disappointment, we can see it in your eyes, and we want to reply, "It is the best we can do," and we need you to acknowledge that with compassion. It would make the pill less bitter for us if we could find some sympathy for that reality. You do not need to rub it in, we feel and experience our weakness, failure and size more than you ever can empathise.'

This unworthiness and lack of truth is a result of the system. With no offence to my fellow clergy, I have over the years gone to several presentations at Deanery Synod meetings where the clergyperson talked up the situation of their own church. I know because I was familiar with all the churches from my many years in the Deanery. I could spot when a photo slide had been focussed on the small group in a large room and not how old they were because I knew them. If the system of assessing church forces the clergy to be dishonest, for fear of censure, the system Is not working.

The CWASC, I believe, gives the best experience of what belonging to a church is. A church with a modest congregation is the hardest to belong to and the most challenging. Nevertheless, it can potentially lead to the greater thirst for God.

Surrendering to who and what we are as a church, liberates us to explore what we should be like as we wait on God. I have never experienced this myself, but I understand that in some poor countries rail links are uncertain and infrequent and that it is not unusual to get to some backwater, rail station to find that your connection will not arrive for a week. There is nothing to do but wait it out. So, churches need patience.

There is plenty to keep us busy - we can develop a rich inner life.

2 Keep my commands and live; protect my teachings as the pupil of your eye. 3 Tie them to your fingers; write them on the tablet of your heart.
4 Say to wisdom, "You are my sister," and call understanding your relative. Proverbs 7:2-4 (CSB).

When I say 'we', I mean the CWASC. Bible studies and prayer meetings can continue, along with all sorts of fellowship groups, to keep hearts and minds busy without the need to feel downcast that our limited numbers mean we are programmed to failure. Where **two or three are gathered**, larger numbers do not mean a larger Jesus or more of his time. Numbers do not buy his fellowship or love. Grace can be experienced in minority as well as majority. It only takes the prayers of a few to create a holy space, or a fellowship activity to encourage all who visit it.

[20] Look at Zion, the city of our festival times. Your eyes will see Jerusalem, a peaceful pasture, a tent that does not wander; its tent pegs will not be pulled up nor will any of its cords be loosened. Isaiah 33:20 (CSB)

We can use our imaginations too. I love the Dinotopia books and the rich drawings of festivals that include humans and dinosaurs. They communicate something rich and powerful. A CWASC can dream of Jerusalem. It can remember – O, remember how important remembrance is in the Scriptures! In the records of my CWASC were photographs of the church in the 1930s that included some amazing pictures of local festivals organised by the church at that time in history when it was the main source of entertainment and social life for the community. These memories are not to be taken as critical of the present, rather, with thankfulness for the church's heritage.

[8] He has only human strength, but we have the LORD our God to help us and to fight our battles." So the people relied on the words of King Hezekiah of Judah. 2 Chron 32:8 (CSB).

It is a time to focus on the strength of God. God is God With A Very Large Number Of Worshippers – GIGWAVLNOW!

The Multiplied Bread

[42] A man from Baal-shalishah came to the man of God with his sack full of twenty loaves of barley bread from the first bread of the harvest. Elisha said, "Give it to the people to eat." [43] But Elisha's attendant asked, "What?

Am I to set twenty loaves before a hundred men?" "Give it to the people to eat," Elisha said, "for this is what the LORD says: 'They will eat, and they will have some left over.'" [44] So he gave it to them, and as the LORD had promised, they ate and had some left over. 2 Kings 4:42-44 (CSB).

Not only should we remember the past, but, despite being forced to wait, we should wait with hope. If you were a traveller and did not believe that your connection would come, you would despair. Anybody who makes a CWASC despair... should have millstone tied around their neck... God can make the few become the many. However, we are not to purge all our own feelings of self-abnegation and unworthiness, that would be pride. After all, we are all unworthy. We are not to punish ourselves for our failures, or allow the critical spirit of others to do so either. Nevertheless, we must accept that God may say a 'No' to us and trust him.

...you give them drink from the river of your delights. Psalms 36:8 (NRSV).

God has many wonderful gifts to give. How often does he say you do not deserve this, but your bigger brother does?

Never.

The prodigal son got all the attention and God reassured the brother who stayed at home that he already has all the inheritance.

There are limits to what a CWASC can do, but it can still do some - and 'be' plenty.

CHAPTER 19 – Presenting The Gospel.

I am writing this on Dec 3rd, a day of memorial for Saint Francis Xavier, Priest, who pursued a missionary calling in several nations including India and China. I was interested in reading one of his letters to Saint Ignatius in which he wrote of his despair at the lack of priests to carry on the work; the huge need this created because of the many who wished to hear the gospel, but were denied the opportunity as there was nobody to teach them. What then follows is Xavier's basic minimum of knowledge to become a Christian after baptism: a confession of faith in the person the Trinity; the Apostles' Creed; the Lord's Prayer and the Hail Mary. Of course, it is not clear whether he was giving teaching behind these historic statements or whether the knowledge of them, even simply by rote, was sufficient. For those of us who want to give potential converts a thorough understanding of the Christian faith before they commit, it seems woefully inadequate. Yet you only need to look no further than our own Book of Common Prayer and the Catechism to see how imperfect and thin was the expected biblical and liturgical knowledge required to a launch a Christian on confirmation and beyond. In fact, candidates only needed to be word perfect and not necessarily comprehending.

Maybe we are too concerned to judge faith in terms of 'knowledge required' before we allow potential converts forward. The early church excluded catechists from Holy Communion until they were mature enough. And my own understanding is not helped by the way in which I became a Christian myself. I was brought up through the Methodist Sunday school system in the 1960s. I distinctly remember being asked to sign the Discipleship Roll at some point and refusing point blank. To be frank I only became a teenage attender because the church had a thriving youth group with a good number of young women in it. It was not until university that I came across a thorough explanation of the gospel. In my case it was supplied by the Rev David McInnes during the triennial university mission. In those days, in the 1970s, it was more of a lecture topped and tailed by a song. There was no intense worship to bookend it or even overt emotionalism. It was very factual and clear and, to me, like a draft of the coolest, purest water, quenching a thirst I did not know existed at that point. Even then I was very cautious and, after finally speaking to a counsellor, made my way back to my university hall of residence room to make a prayer of commitment in private. The consequence was powerful, for I woke the next day knowing Jesus was with me, a feeling that has never left me since 1973.

Clearly for me an intellectual understanding of faith was paramount before I could move forward. It is easy in those situations to think that this is the way, the only way. However, it is one of the privileges of ministry to be party to many more confessions of faith in private, pastoral moments than most people hear. It soon became clear that there is no definitive path to Christ. There is a wonderful spectrum: from those who always knew from early childhood, who seem to have been gifted with the sense of the supernatural presence of Jesus from their mother's milk onwards, to those who struggle throughout their lives with immense doubts, who vacillate in and out of faith depending on the prevailing winds of their lives' experiences. I was privilege to baptise one of my own churchwardens who, at an advanced age, attended one of my basic Christian courses and found Jesus for the first time after a lifetime of church attendance and went on to make a powerful testimony of it at the baptism itself.

Clearly, not everyone enters through the intellectual door. However, I cannot completely deny the truth that some understanding of the facts must be an essential part of coming to Christ, or certainly finding an adult faith. Why else would Paul say there is not faith without hearing? Notice he did not say there is no faith without understanding. Again, long years of ministry will show repeatedly that even the most basic teaching does not stick in some people's minds.

'Oh, why was I not taught this before,' someone might say, 'after all these years at church it is completely new to me.'

Well, I distinctly remember saying something similar last year and will no doubt say it again next. I record this with affection. Many of those who made this plea were the finest Christians I know. 'Getting it' is not everything.

On the other hand, I have suffered years of having to attend the most banal of church functions which seemed bereft of any Christian content in what I believe was the mistaken belief that it would get people into church. My own aversion to flower festivals was formed, when, as a brand-new curate, I was forced by my boss to attend the whole weekend long flower festival, in order to be present and to engage with the visitors. Now I am not decrying taking opportunities to get people into church, but a flower festival on Hollywood Movies to my mind does not 'cut the mustard'. And even my presence as curiosity – the new curate - did not, as far as I can ascertain, provoke any conversions. Equally, being too triumphalist can be off putting to many of a more sensitive constitution. I recall attending a tragic funeral, following as consequence on the death of a young person. Her own church congregation chose to celebrate her new life in heaven at the expense of the palpable sense of bereavement of a vast number of her secular friends, who were quite bewildered that their own sense of loss, which stemmed from their own life experience - an understand that their friend was dead and gone – was omitted. It was far too evangelistic to be piggy-backed on such a sensitive event.

A good mix of peripheral, attractive, church-lite activities is most likely to bear fruit when it comes to charming people to central church events. This in turn will lead to the opportunity to hear a clear explanation of the gospel, in a non-judgemental setting, and thus opportunities to make a commitment. This is only the beginning; clear systematic teaching must follow. If we read the Acts of the Apostles, although it seems that Paul and the other apostles had some great early success in bringing people to Christ, they prudently followed it up with months, even years of teaching, service opportunities and the appointment of elders to pastor the church, even sending pointed letters from afar.

The CWASC finds itself in a unique position: often isolated, few in number, but in communities like villages where its members are known and scrutinised; or desolate, urban situations where the community sees them as no more than wraiths, who disappear occasionally into large forbidding, almost derelict, church buildings.

The country mice may indeed run the flower festivals and fairs, struggling to know how to Christianise their parish in its prevailing secular culture. The town mice must rely on good works and kindness. These are both good foundations that need craftsperson like work to continue.

I can offer no formulae to how to do this. To my mind it must always begin with an enquiry directed to God as to what he wants to do.

In my own suburban situation, I once heard God's voice as I left church and headed to the lych-gate say, 'I am not calling many disciples in this generation.' Rather than be a cold, damp cloth and a reinforcement of my desire, in my low moments, to give up, I found it an incredible relief. I could stop beating myself up for once at my failure to get the church to thrive and expand. Unless the Lord was to help build the house of my church my energies would be wasted.

15b This is what the LORD says: 'Do not be afraid or discouraged because of this vast number, for the battle is not yours, but God's.

17 You do not have to fight this battle. Position yourselves, stand still, and see the salvation of the LORD. He is with you, Judah and Jerusalem. Do not be afraid or discouraged. Tomorrow, go out to face them, for Yahweh is with you.'" 2 Chronicles 20:15b & 17 (CSB).

And from the pre-crossing of the Red Sea.

13 But Moses said to the people, "Do not be afraid. Stand firm and see the LORD'S salvation He will provide for you today; for the Egyptians you see today, you will

never see again. [14] The LORD will fight for you; you must be quiet." Exodus 14:13-14 (CSB).

Both speak of the adversity faced by the Hebrews from an enemy of superior strength. Fortunately for us in this country, the large forces of unbelievers are not at this moment against us, only indifferent. It is too early to develop a bunker mentality about persecution when there is very little and where indifference and its depressive consequence is more effective.

Many will feel that 'stand still and be quiet' does not seem the best strategy for a CWASC. It is though, if it gives God space to act on their behalf. We will all have seen slapstick comedy where a small, short man is held at bay by a bigger man with longer arms; simply by putting his hand on the small man's head he can keep him at arm's length. Being quiet and still gives us a longer reach, and a chance to reflect on our own dignity. Let us not sell the gospel cheaply, even for the sake of kindness and charity. Although, I believe it is disingenuous to offer kindness in order to lead people on and not explain to them the punchline. Some of you will know the two bears in a bath non-joke!

Shotgun charities of the past used to gather street people in to a chapel and then harangued them for an hour before they were given anything to eat. Simply giving somebody something to eat and not explaining your motivation for doing so is surely as bad. When a church looks too much like a secular institution it will confuse people. They will not get by osmosis that it was because Jesus dies on a cross for them that we are offering social care. I can understand that in situations where it is forbidden to preach the gospel then any means must be used, any kind act can communicate something of God, but whilst we have the freedom, we must say the words too. [Of course, God can work supernaturally, converting by his revealed presence alone, but it seems more normative that the good news is spoken to provoke a response.]

...man does not live on bread alone but on every word that comes from the mouth of the LORD. Deuteronomy 8:3 (CSB).

Jesus himself spoke of the wrong reason for the crowds following him – they wanted to be fed again like before and were satisfied with the bread alone and not with him. He gave Satan short shrift during his temptation, recorded in Mathew and Luke, by using the quote above. We must find some middle ground on which to stand still and be quiet. I suspect God will show us a particular strategy for our church and even if he does not, we must still be busy with the work of the kingdom in our midst. [33] **But seek first the kingdom of God and his righteousness, and all these things will be provided for you.** Matthew 6:33 (CSB). We have been given a perpetual Biblical Warrant by Jesus to begin with this.

As we have already noted, the church has a set of peculiar gifts and peculiar disabilities. Almost like a real person! There is more than one way to skin a cat, they say. You will think me cowardly for not suggesting specific strategies, but I know if I do, I might undermine the voice of God to you, when you are still and quiet. Here though, as illustrations, are two examples. Firstly, they need to be shown that as great as liturgical prayer is on a Sunday, it is different from individual and corporate prayer. Maybe this is the point to start. Sadly, in some cases, CWASCs, weakened by long years of neglect and possibly poor teaching, do not know some of the basic skills. The congregation may never have experienced the joy of meeting in a group and praying together in the week, or been taught how to pray by themselves and to keep a prayer diary, even for the church to set a subject for prayer and then to review them regularly to see how they are going.

And, here is an idea for this Sunday, a variation: announce a topic for prayer from the pulpit. Ask your congregation to pray about it each day. Tell them, 'If you have trouble knowing how to pray here is one I wrote earlier. [A copy is handed out at the church door.] Please say it every day and sit quiet and still afterwards and try to hear what God is saying. Write down anything that comes to you and put the answer in the box next Sunday. However weird or strange the answer is, even if it is adream, or it was provoked by a TV programme you were watching, write it down and bring it to church.'

6 **Listen, for I speak of noble things,**
and what my lips say is right. Proverbs 8:6 (CSB).

It is the beginning of a journey. Who knows when we will arrive? Surely, teaching people to pray and listen to God, and be still and quiet, is a milepost that all churches need to pass with their congregations?

And what is ahead in the journey? What are those other mileposts? Well in the light of this passage one must surely be having an evangelistic event of some sort. I know as I type those words it will bring back memories of Billy Graham or J.John events. I am not talking about those. Something my church has tried is getting people to video a short testimony and put it on Facebook. Bingo. That's an evangelistic event! And do not stop being kind and charitable also, or even having flower festivals, but find a way that during them they may reflect the true nature and purpose of the church in which they bloom.

CHAPTER 20 - Its Good Heart.

[50] **Remember, Lord, the ridicule against your servants — in my heart I carry abuse from all the peoples —** [51] **how your enemies have ridiculed, LORD, how they have ridiculed every step of your anointed.** Psalms 89:50-51 (CSB).

Is a CWASC anointed?

Why is it that we think a CWASC is numerically challenged and financially poor because of their own bad choices? This is a common meme in society, usually applied to the feelings that rich people have about poor people, but no less applicable in a church comparison situation. When Jesus was asked if the man born blind was a sinner, he rejected the judgment immediately responding...

[3] **"Neither this man nor his parents sinned," Jesus answered. "This came about so that God's works might be displayed in him.** John 9:3 (CSB).

Behind these false judgments lies the psychological concept known as 'fundamental attribution error'. This is a natural tendency to see the behaviour of others as being determined by their own character – while excusing our own behaviour based on circumstance. It is a matter of point of view. For example, a CWASC might see itself as a victim of circumstances beyond its control, stuck in a financial environment caused by the country's economic situation that made it impossible for the young people of the community to find a job with a living wage, and to find affordable accommodation. It may be the long-term sickness of their incumbent that is the limiting factor, or a high percentage of emotionally damaged, yet demanding and strongminded people in the congregation in positions of leadership. It could be undisclosed sin in an individual, etc., Those ignorant of such a history find it all too easy to describe such churches as weak and failing, discounting the faults of their own situation.

That is certainly true in my experience: it is always much easier to judge from a distance, without the facts and certainly without any empathy. What bothers me more is not the lack of self-understanding in those who make such judgments, but in the structures of the church that bring consequences in the wake of such conclusions. Why is it felt necessary to poke such congregations and their ministries with a stick? Any self-respecting minister, who is committed and hardworking will only too easily hold themselves to account for the failings of their churches. They really do not need anybody to come and beat them up about it at the same time. If, despite the circumstances of a church, they have managed to retain or gain a measure of self-respect and contentment, why is there any need to destroy that? If we are told that the poor will always be with us. Why then is it so difficult to treat them with compassion? Leave the poor alone, they do not need censure, they need appropriate help.

It is of course more subtle in a church. It is not so much: they obviously did not try too hard at that last stewardship campaign or they would not be in this fix. The criticism can quickly spread to a judgment about their theology, church style or lack of evangelism, all often narrowly defined by the critics in any case. Even if the CWASC practises humility, something that the divine Thomas a Kempis recommends, to turn away the anger of critics, it does not stop the condemnation. Somebody will always want to put you right.

Another attitude we find among the rich:

'I deserve all this money because I worked hard. Therefore, the poor, because they do not have any money, must have not worked very hard.' The false logic of this is breathtaking. Personally, I suspect that very rich people can only have become so by doing down the poor somewhere along the line. They have fallen into the trap of Nebuchadnezzar. He got up one day, surveyed all he had and ascribed his success to himself. Bad choice. It was only when he was humbled and accepted that all the good things he enjoyed came from God's blessing, and not related to any natural talents or assets he possessed, that he was redeemed.

The rich are rich largely because of good fortune and the poor are poor because of bad fortune. Despite their efforts they mostly remain so. The church situation brings out the subtlety. Well, actually, not very subtle.

'Our church is so big and thriving because we did it right. It is down to our efforts, our mission statement and plan etc., If other churches follow what we do the same will happen to them. It is a take on the Prosperity Gospel, where success is measured in spiritual acumen and not cash.

The thing that provokes the use of a stick to prod a CWASC is the money and the cost of ministry. Some CWALCs have complained that they should not, through the parish share, have to support the CWASCs. Why not? Nobody wants to answer that. A look in the NT and a study of Paul's lessons to congregations about stumping up for those in need would prove instructive. And why should a CWALC, this is the worst bit to them, give cash that is just going to be handed to CWASCs that are not pulling their weight, or worse, not even on the same page when it comes to how to worship God or run a church? This reveals an incredible amount of pride and condescension that is unworthy of the church if it is called to one body.

It is why a country would not feel able to be generous with the poor, because - they do not deserve it and would waste it - they are not worthy! I have tried in many ways during this paper to explain why a CWASC might be worthy in God's eyes, and in some cases even more worthy than a CWALC. And if such a church finds a degree of contentment, why should we rob them of it to teach them a lesson?

If this issue could be resolved then I feel there would be a lot less friction. And a CWASC would be allowed to police itself. I have not suggested a CWASC is to be permitted to lower its standards in any way, but rather to be bolstered in its self-worth. For it is that, in itself, that will work wonders.

In his book *Freedom of Simplicity* Richard Foster sings the praises of God's generosity, not only the spiritual but the physical as well. In the NT we find that Jesus expands this Godly generosity to an encouragement to us to be liberal to others. When he sends out the seventy-two ahead of him, he tells these disciples to stay with those who welcome them and who show them goodwill. No judgements beyond this are to be made. They are to stay where God puts them. It is beholden on the CWALC to treat the CWASC with as much goodwill as vice versa.

Dare I suggest that God seems more concerned with Christians, and with churches, being good to each other, rather than prioritising finding more members. Is it possible that unlocking the problem of the lack of Christian unity might have a more powerful effect in growing the church than any number of evangelistic outreach programmes? There is a general call in Scripture to overgenerosity to other Christians and churches.

And remember: those who manage their own households well first then find themselves given more responsibility for others.

5 **(If anyone does not know how to manage his own household, how will he take care of God's church?)** 1 Timothy 3:5 (CSB).

Not least the household of faith.

10 Therefore, as we have opportunity, let us work for the good of all, **especially for those who belong to the household of faith**. Galatians 6:10 (CSB).

Given the circumstances the heart of a CWASC is often sound even if the body itself is disabled or challenged in its witness. Repeatedly we have seen that God's love for a church is not measured by the physicality of what we may see in a church. How good that God does not judge by appearance. We have something to learn from that.

50 Remember, Lord, the ridicule against your servants — in my heart I carry abuse from all the peoples — 51 how your enemies have ridiculed, LORD, how they have ridiculed every step of your anointed. Psalms 89:50-51(CSB).

Psalm 89 is a Maskill of Ethan the Ezrahite. This song is set in the time of King David and the psalm is a response to the fallen fortunes of the king in the face of catastrophes. The psalmist reminds God of his contractual obligations, so to speak, towards David and his kingdom. The psalm draws to a close with our chosen verses when Ethan reminds God that David and Israel are God's servants and David is his anointed. You chose us Lord, Ethan reminds God. The verses are the Christian Study Bible's attempts to make sense of this ungrammatical plea. CWASCs always have the option to call out to God. Whereas the critics might want them to call out to God for a renewal of chutzpah, faith, commitment and everything they think is missing in the church, the CWASC knows that its first prayer is to call out against those who have become its enemies and to keep a good heart.

CHAPTER 21 - Its Past, Present – Hard Pressed & Future Dreams.

From Balaam's poem in his fourth oracle:

21 **Next he saw the Kenites and proclaimed his poem: Your dwelling place is enduring; your nest is set in the cliffs.** Num 24:21 (CSB)

I find it very difficult to distinguish between my dreams, my ambitions, the longing of my heart and most importantly my calling to ministry. I have experienced two 'calls' in my life. The first to ordained ministry in the Church of England and the second, coming shortly after I was ordained, to write novels. My ordained ministry as a parish priest has now transmogrified into the ministry of retired priest on PTO and my writing career continues. If I am alone in the following statement, then things are worse than I feared, but along with being called to ordained ministry I definitely felt I was called to 'successful ordained ministry'. I do not think it crossed my mind at first that it might not be so. It was not until I began my first incumbency, after two curacies, that I began to realise it might not be completely up to me. When I began preaching as a Methodist lay preacher, and for many years afterwards, I arrogantly, now I see, believed that my every sermon would be world shattering and people-changing. By the time of my retirement from stipendiary ministry, I likened myself to a radio station that was always on in the back ground, that none of the church members could turn off. And my ambitions for my church to come alive, based on a constant searching to get it right and find the exact form of words, or the exact church-growth strategy, ended abruptly when a major schism in my church, not I believe of my making, set back the church for several years and left a residue forever.

It was during these hard years that I began to ask God why he had sent me to farm such a stony field. At least I was beginning to accept it was not my fault. By the end of my ministry, and, although there was the natural slowing of age, I do not think I had let up on my hopes and dreams. I reached a more sober estimate of what I could achieve in such a situation where there were so many factors beyond my control. I never lost the sense that God, by clicking his fingers, could make it so different and flood the church with people eager to receive the gospel, who would do so, and then step immediately into all sorts of exciting ministry - but I did not expect it even though I hoped for it. By the end I walked away with a sense that I had given it my best shot, that although the church was numerically less than when I began – it just so happened my ministry coincided with a catastrophic growth of indifference in society and drop in numbers of church goers - I felt content that I would be able to answer for what I had done and not what my exertions had achieved. Now I have a new ministry in a different parish where I am no longer in charge, seeing it all play out again, as it does time and time again in churches.

I found easier to surrender to these dreams and ambitions for my spiritual ministry than my second call to write secular fiction. This has been a far rockier road and with more testing: tempting dreams about what fame might come my way by being discovered as a new voice, or becoming a famous writer whose readers waited with anticipation for each new book to arrive at Waterstones.

All this is of course part of growing old. The certainties and arrogance of youth, hopefully, are abraded by life. In time we come to that gentler understanding of our worth. I recall as a younger clergyman being a bit nonplussed by the cavalier and almost negligent attitude of the older guys who seemed rather cynical about it all – tried that, done that. Now I am in that age group I have learnt to keep my mouth shut and rejoice in the burst of enthusiasm that young clergy bring to our church.

As we have already noted it is important to remember the history of a church, at the same time not forgetting that for a CWASC, even though life might be hard pressed, there is still room for dreams of a different future. Often these dreams have centred around their desire for a younger clergyperson with family and young children to revive the work among children, young people and stay-at-home partners and families. The train has left the station of that desire: as already noted dioceses presently plan their children's work around church schools. There is no magic bullet that will restore it all to its glory days. This is the lesson: not to get our dreams in a twist with our past! Rather, allow God to inform our dreams - and to use our common sense! It is not wrong to long for our CWASC to become a CWALC, but we must not be so consumed by it that we refuse to do anything until it becomes so. There is plenty to do in a CWASC, and if we can remove the stigma of being such a church, and take joy in the small gains and the challenges overcome, our dreams might come true. We cannot remain forever optimistic that God will intervene and do all the work for us. For my entire Christian ministry, I have come repeatedly against groups who have proclaimed that God was doing a great thing in that generation and there would be a palpable and wholesale turning to God. Where is it? I see no evidence of it.

There is a difference between dreams and fantasy. Dreams are to be tested; fantasy is too slippery for such rigour. Dreams are to be tested against Scripture, against the wisdom of mature Christians, weathered with a healthy dose of pragmatism, intuition and common sense, and a final measure of worldly wisdom is not to be eschewed.

21 Next he saw the Kenites and proclaimed his poem: Your dwelling place is enduring; your nest is set in the cliffs. Numbers 24:21 (CSB).

We find the Kenites in the OT. They were not of the people of Israel, but found acceptance by them. Moses' father-in-law, who proved so helpful, was a Kenite. They may be descended from Cain. They were a tribe of metal workers. King Saul helped them to escape a slaughter because of the help they had given Israel in the wilderness:

Saul warned the Kenites, "Since you showed kindness to all the Israelites when they came out of Egypt, go on and leave! Get away from the Amalekites, or I'll sweep you away with them." So the Kenites withdrew from the Amalekites. 1 Samuel 15:6 (CSB).

Our Chapter heading verse from Numbers shows the beginning of the Kenites connection with the Israelites in that they are mentioned in the Prophecy of Balaam's fourth oracle. What a beautiful metaphor he speaks. Those of you who have read my book *Honey from the*

Rock will know my love of these phrases and metaphors of Scripture that do not add or detract from any doctrine we may wish to establish, but simply embellish the text and bring joy to the heart.

Can we say that the CWASC feels like the Kenites at times: useful to the people of God, yet tolerated and sometimes despised?

Can there be any more worthy dream as this for a CWASC - a place of safety and endurance as a church in face of life's problems.

And if it be true who would not be drawn to such a place of safety and security?

CHAPTER 22 - Love In A CWASC.

[1] The LORD is my shepherd; there is nothing I lack. Psalms 23:1 (HCSB).

One of the elements of my ministerial training was a counselling course. This involved, on occasions, role play. The one I was invited to model was an elderly couple who were about to be married, but were anxious, as they were both virgins, about consummating their marriage. As it happened, as a married man myself, having been married at 22 and by now in my thirties, I had something to say. The lecturer kindly gave me some praise for the way I had handled it. I can't remember what I said exactly, but it was along the lines of what an adventure they were about to begin on and that there was no correct way and that I was sure once they relaxed about it, they would find a really nice way to please each other.

In our modern, digital world love has become conflated with sex and sex has become an Olympic event. What harm this does to impressionable young minds and enflames the insensitive to treat each other badly is yet to be revealed. Although love has a sexual component, it is not defined by it and probably, in more cases than we hear about, is absent in some committed, loving relationships. Phew. That takes the pressure off. It is handy to have love defined in 1 Cor 13 and in Romans 15, but these are not checklists or blueprints, and neither do they take account of the fact that love changes over the years. My love for my wife of 45 years and its expression has changed over the course of our marriage. I certainly do not love my wife in the same way I loved my parents, my children, my friends or even my favourite fountain pen. English is so limited by having only that single word love

Cleary then we are not going to find a homogenous consensus as to what love might look like in a CWASC. I have tended to describe the CWASC as a church with an elderly congregation mainly because I have been trying to defend small congregations against the worst of the pejorative judgements they attract. However, as a working description it is a poor generalisation. CWASCs are not unvaryingly elderly nor do they express their love with any lack of vigour or generosity. What is common is that love is not a performance. We can all spot when somebody is trying too hard. The root of trying to understand this is, as always, overcoming the fixed notions that some people carry that they know what love is and anybody who strays from their definition is wrong. I have always been intrigued, when observing people through many pastoral engagements, what it is that glues some couples together, especially when to my mind one of them seems to be deeply unpleasant to the other. Accepting of course psychological problems like co-dependency, etc. the only explanation where this is absent must be a love beyond my comprehension.

One of the most impressive examples of love I came across in a church was to be found in my ladies' group. This was a collection of ladies, mostly widowed, in their late 70s, numbering about 15. The weekly meeting was like the tip of the iceberg. It was quite simplistic and charming and beneath the surface ran a deep current of care. They all knew when each other was ill as they kept in touch by telephone. One of the leaders was an indefatigable visitor who, like a bee carried the pollen of her findings, from house to house. Birthdays and special occasions were remembered, cards and presents given. Were they evangelists for the church? Not in the way that has become defined. Were they witnesses – absolutely! Did they generate much heat for the world to see? None to the worldly. Yet how wonderful it was.

Love is moulded and expressed by the interests of the love giver. Another elderly friend, when introduced to the idea of Amnesty International, took to it like duck to water, eventually leaving the bulk of her estate to them when she died.

The love of Christ is sometimes the equivalent of eros in the young Christian, but later in life is most often without passion and more often expressed as the pragmatic every week, every day the same, sort of love that takes immense energy to promote and sustain. It is beyond exciting and new.

I am puzzled by churches that advertise everything they do as a new initiative. All of it seems to be novel and exciting. If they are not careful, they start a new initiative and a few months later start a new on. If the old one was worth doing, it was worth continuing...continuously worth doing. Churches only have limited capacity and if this 'constantly being moved on to new projects' operates, then the old, worthy projects - well they were when they were new and exciting - will have to be dumped. This inevitably will look unloving to the first set of beneficiaries.

Love is steady and faithful. It does not change through the years and each church must find its own way of expressing it internally and externally. Obviously, as a church reduces in size and ages then its capabilities diminish. This is something that the surrounding churches need to recognise, and even those outside the church, in the parish itself, must come to terms with.

I was recently reading the lovely hymn of praise to the people of God that we find in psalm 23. The commentary flagged up: 'he guides me along the right path,' as, 'you lead you people along safe paths.' It was a revelation. Suddenly my mind was flooded with the image of refugees being led from one country to another during the height of WW2 across mountains along safe routes by local guides, so they did not come into danger. Suddenly the psalm made a whole new sense to me.

'Yes of course, God's love for me is like the experienced mountain guide leading me along a safe path where I will avoid danger.'

This surely is love: using all our local knowledge and experience to lead those temporarily entrusted to us, our congregation, members of our parish community, to safety.

Love is thriving in the CWASCs. It appears more reserved than emotional, if the congregation is elderly, yet in reality it is like a deep running river that deserves its due respect and honour.

CHAPTER 23 - Its Parish Expectations.

[22] **Do not be afraid of them, for the LORD your God fights for you.** Deuteronomy 3:22 (CSB).

The church building in my last incumbency had stood on the top of a small rise since 1301. Occasionally, parishioners living within half a mile of the building, and, who I guessed were long term residents, asked me where the church building was. They were surprised when I told them, as they had never once been down the road that led to it, even to get to the popular walks over the marshes beyond it.

The parish can be indifferent to their parish church and often do not see any connection between themselves and it. The church of course, to them, is not the people who worship there, but only ever the building! However, when people want the church, they really want it and it becomes theirs in ways that are inappropriate. When they do not it is as if it does not even exist; they give it less than no thought.

When they really want the church building, especially if they want it to remain as it is, regardless as to whether it serves any practical purpose, they will fight tooth and nail to get it to remain as it is in their imagination, whilst steadfastly refusing to darken its door. During my ministry, at least two local churches met with quite vocal and spiteful opposition over the proposed removal of pews. I suspect this is not such a keen issue nowadays, as society has moved on to a degree: first generation, disconnected worshippers have become second and third; there has been a consequent loss of interest. In fact, where churches have stepped in to host Post Offices, or cleared their pews to host community events, even hiring out their buildings, this generated good will rather than rancour.

Others want their church building to be at their disposal. All clergy will have received a call from parishioner asking to hire the building for a wedding. And they seem puzzled when I would tease them by asking if it was only the building they want, or whether my presence was required to marry them. Certainly, any latent respect for the building has largely evaporated. After one christening – the popular description – when I came back from the door, where I had been saying goodbye to guests, I found the mother of the baby, an amateur photographer, laying the baby on the communion table and moving around the furniture to provide a suitable back drop for her photos. Any sense that the building might be a holy space has disappeared for many. I had to turn down psychic investigators who wished to spend a night vigil in the church. After explaining that the church was very definitely the congregation, and that the special atmosphere inside the church was the product of centuries of worship and prayer and thus best left alone, they became puzzled.

The most aggressive behaviour seems to be provoked by an open graveyard. The explanation that the rules of the CofE for its graveyards were quite different from a municipal cemetery, seemed to inflame grieving relatives to heights of rage and provoke complicated attempts to overturn such rules.

Blessedly, there are those who have an encounter with the church, the building even, who are intrigued and grateful for the experience. Generally wedding couples, baptism families and bereaved relatives, if treated appropriately, although remaining ignorant of the subtleties of what happened to them through the occasional offices, are touched by the experience and retain an openness to further ministry and an appropriate affection for the building. When I needed to build an inside toilet for the church, my master file of contacts, culled from these occasional offices, provided, on renewed contact, a substantial sum of money for the project; I appealed to their sense of gratitude about what they had received from the church and wondered if they might help us to continue and provide better facilities in the future. Result!

However, it is right to recognise that often in tiny villages, the community grew around the church when it was built and it provided a focus. I have mentioned how my own church in the 1930 was a hub of all things social for the community.

The CWASC must remain humble in its attitude to the parish, yet confident. God is on their side; nothing can harm them. They have something of inestimable value to give everyone in their parish. The building is indeed a parish church and not the church's building alone. All are welcome, but are rightly encouraged to be respectful. The building is important to many people, not least the church congregation. Much love, well remembered, is recorded within its walls: the struggle to buy a new boiler; the stained glass in memory of N. Questions and enquires must be answered thoroughly and kindly. Invitations to real events, not just summer fayres, but to actual services are to be an integral part of the churches service to the community.

The writer of Ecclesiastes gives timely advice: the parish can be a curse and a blessing.

[21] Do not pay attention to everything people say, or you may hear your servant cursing you, [22] for in your heart you know that many times you yourself have cursed others. Ecclesiastes 7:21-22 (CSB).

It is easy to berate the hot and cold attitude of the parish, their inability to get it and their false and harmful enthusiasms to protect the building unaltered. Nevertheless, the church as its congregation is vicarious.

'Say one for me,' people sometimes say.

And are surprised when we say, 'Of course.'

These prayers get answered, although rarely ascribed to God's direct action. Ministry in parishes is wearing for all and for the committed Christian will sound like Moses:

[22] {Zipporah} gave birth to a son whom {Moses} named Gershom [a stranger there], for he said, **"I have become a resident alien in a foreign land."** Ex 2:22 (CSB).

This sometimes tense dislocation between parish community and parish building, the church, can give an alien view of the landscape around the church. As Christians we are citizens of heaven inducted into a heavenly kingdom, unseen except in the unique, physical presence of the church building at its most.

It is good to remember that the strangers in Israel were often the slaves and servants of the community. As resident aliens in our parish we are called to no less.

CHAPTER 24 – It is The Lord's Doing Ultimately.

17 I love those who love me, and those who search for me find me. Prov 8:17 (CSB).

2 For I am jealous for you with a godly jealousy, because I have promised you in marriage to one husband—to present a pure virgin to Christ. 2 Corinthians 11:2 (CSB).

When Paul writes to the Corinthian church, he is not writing to the Church Universal. He is writing to one specific congregation and he talks about the emotions he feels as a kind of bride's father as he presents the church to her new husband Christ. We are given this image to extrapolate into other similar situations. Although Christ is the head and the husband of the Church Universal it is not wrong to see individual churches, whether they be CWASCs or CWALCs, in such an intimate relationship. In fact, once again, there seems to be no numerical limitations to this metaphor.

The anointing of a church is quite independent from the way we as humans tend to measure these things. If holiness was based on capital, then Jeff Bezos would be one of the holiest people on earth at this moment, and if it were based on size, then his organisation Amazon would be a shining beacon of sanctity. In the topsy turvy world of Christianity the poor widow, who put her last coin into the treasury, is the holiest and the poorest churches, often in third world countries, the brightest light in the ecclesiastical heavens.

It is so important that we do finally banish such unworthy thoughts and judgments from our mind as we try to second guess who God might favour, based on our own prejudices as to how we measure success.

God addresses the patriarch Abram, before even his name has changed, at the very beginning of his dependant walk with him:

[2] I will make you into a great nation, I will bless you, I will make your name great, and you will be a blessing. [3] I will bless those who bless you, I will curse those who treat you with contempt, and all the peoples on earth will be blessed through you. Gen 12:2-3 (CSB).

The success of the enterprise of Abram's life and his resulting dynastic heritage is entirely in the hands and gift of God. Abram came under the direct interest and protection of God.

Serendipity is super charged by God's blessing and the destruction of those who resist him. One day the whole earth will know the truth. One day the whole heaven will know the truth of some of these CWASCs that have been side-lined and dismissed. Justice will be done. None of us, not one of our churches, is secure in anything we base on our own arrogance. Everything built on such a foundation will be swept away in the final judgment of God. The only thing left standing will be God's willed heritage, all else sluiced away by the blood of the cross.

There was nothing obvious about Abram, to those of his day, that made them think his name would even be remembered thousands of years later, let alone celebrated. He embarked upon a spiritual pilgrimage so perilous that he almost fell at the first hurdle - a son, Isaac, who did not come until well past the last moment for two old bodied parents.

We need to look constantly to God for his discernment; for an ability to look at what the world, and even our natural state, labels as unpromising and see it with his eyes. I wonder what would happen if society swept away, by legal decrees, the obvious expressions of Christianity, as to which form might it survive. Would it be like the flame of a small, tea light guttering in the force of such a strong wind? Would the CWALCs survive such an onslaught, or would they be the more obvious targets for a state determined to wipe out faith? Perhaps it would still survive in the corners of an old building, those in the urban situations, small village or the homes of such.

None of it would survive if God did not desire such a future for them as he did for Abram all those years ago.

17 I love those who love me, and those who search for me find me. Prov 8:17 (CSB).

This is how God responds to a church. This is how God measures the success of a church. It is a lesson for all of us. Our desire for God both individually and corporately provokes a response in him, all the rest is detail. How to search for God – that is a whole new book!

Most of my searching is desperate hunting for lost things or memories. I recently lost the bunch of keys that opened not only our shed but also our back door. I tracked the keys mentally to exactly when I believed I had last used them, to where I usually put the keys and still could not find them. All sorts of desperate thoughts reamed through me including the unknown robber who had somehow got in our garden and stolen them while my back was turned. Until they turned up the search was punctuated with recriminations against myself for being so stupid, but also an intense focus on the places where they might have been mislaid, and the highways and byways of my own brain, as I tried to wrestle from it any new information.

We have all seen police dramas where they search houses and the consequent detailed and focussed forensic investigation that follows. What a contrast to, 'Oh I guess it will turn up someday!' or, 'If I need to know it will present itself.' However, most of our earthly searching is half-hearted. The writers of the book of Proverbs calls us to use some energy and effort.

There are many ways to search for God, but the one that seems particularly to be flagged up by the Scripture is the search of the Scripture, the continuous intervention of God's words in dialogue with our souls. One can never call oneself serious in searching for God without a love and fascination for Scripture. You must find your own way to do it. There are all sorts of aids to help you, or you just start with a Bible and a highlighter - and perhaps a notebook. Scripture is the most marvellous book in its hesitancy to reveal its deeper meaning. There is a resistance within it that encourages more effort, like a hill that gets progressively steeper. Cursory reading will not bring out its flavour. It is not like being a professional tea taster – one sip, a swill and spit it out. You need to have a good working knowledge of it for your mind to start suggesting those humbling connections. Though, I do not believe it is all the mind - it is God's Spirit too. As generous as the Holy Spirit is, I do not think he will give you a supernatural knowledge of parts of the Bible you have never read, except in rare instances: he wants you to put some graft in! What he is more likely to do is, when you are reading Revelation, find something to say about it in psalms – or at least in the psalms you know. And not necessarily the psalms you can quote from line by line. That has never been my forte. With a concordance, Google and often only a vague impression of a short phrase, I can track down most of those barely remembered verses which suddenly have an almost magical relationship with the passage I am reading – how generous God is to use my poor knowledge and even reward me for it. It causes no harm to write out by long hand a particular phrase that stands out. My own quirk is that I love the metaphors of the Scripture and, as soon as I read 'such and such was like', I pause and flesh out with my imagination the metaphor of Scripture. Searching is painstaking, visceral and intellectual work. Although I have said intellectual, it does not mean we have to have qualifications. Scripture is an equal opportunity revealer. And sometimes it takes the simple and uneducated to grasp the most - the uneducated of the world come into their own when it comes to searching Scripture. Education can get in the way.

...the testimony of the LORD is sure, making wise the simple. Psalms 19:7b (KJV).

How does a church search for God in a way that they will find God – his wisdom - according to his promise? By sheer determination. Some of the most blessed and moving church experiences I have had have been in small groups sharing and studying Scripture together. Far from pooling our ignorance it has given the shy and humble voices the opportunity to come out with some tremendous gems.

Let us not forget that God is not an algorithm when it comes to rewarding and fulfilling his promises. We are encouraged to make progress in these things so that it is obvious to everyone. I believe that congregations that exhibit some genuine searching for God, in the individual lives of the Christians of the fellowship, will find a definite improvement in the congregational attitude to its worship and service, such that the signs will not be just obvious to God, but obvious to visitors to the church as well. How does a church, whatever its size, get a good atmosphere and a palpable one? By the quality of the lives of the individual Christians that make it up. This is open to churches of all sizes.

So, back to Paul:

2 For I am jealous for you with a godly jealousy, because I have promised you in marriage to one husband—to present a pure virgin to Christ. 2 Corinthians 11:2 (CSB).

This will be taken up by our next section on ministry, yet it is good to remember that these are not simply Paul's words, they are also those of God the Father, God the Son and God the Holy Spirit too.

This is how God measures the success of any church especially the CWASC:

'I have a son and I wanted him to find a wonderful wife. A natural feeling for fathers do not you agree? And he did! He made a very wise choice and I couldn't have wished for a better daughter-in-law.'

A church is not a machine, or a factory; it is a personality, a warm beating heart.

CHAPTER 25 – As Being Is > Doing, Showing Is > Telling.

29 Jesus replied, "This is the work of God—that you believe in the one he has sent."
John 6:29 (CSB).

What does Jesus want from us? That is really the most important question we need to ask as we seek to serve God in our daily lives. It comes way before, 'What do I want to do for God?' or, 'God do you think this is a good idea?'

This verse comes in the section directly after Jesus' miracle of walking on the water. The crowd, surprised by his disappearance after feeding them, had followed around the lake and tracked him down. It is clear from the passage that Jesus is aware that they are motivated by 'cupboard love'. They want something from him. They want more food. In my text, Jesus tells them very clearly that what he wants from them [and us] is not primarily doing but being. Believing in the one who God has sent has a passive, internal sense to it.

It seems to suggest that the foundation of the Christian life begins and sometimes ends entirely within our heart, mind and spirit.

I used to ponder what would happen to my ministry if I became so severely disabled that I was unable to do anything for God at all. I imagined what it would be like to be one of those poor, unfortunate people who are called 'locked-in'. It has only recently been discovered that a few people who were taken to be in a coma have really had a rich, aware, inner life, even though they could not move a single muscle, or even appear conscious at all. Would it be possible to live an authentic Christian life if this were the case? If you were unable to do anything physical, any act of service at all, could you still live a Christian life in which God would be satisfied? The answer from my text must be, 'yes', completely. Jesus requires us **first** to 'be well' for him rather than 'do well' for him.

Our most common fault is to think that Christianity is quite the reverse of this, that God would have us so active as his servants that we finally become some sort of Christian machine, doing and doing, and that's enough. The problem with beginning with doing is that we reserve our internal life, our thoughts, emotions and fantasies entirely to ourselves. Thus, our doing becomes disconnected from any deep and meaningful relationship with God and returns to the private life of a non-Christian. This doing rather than being can become addictive. Our preferred lifestyle becomes, 'I did not have time to check this out thoroughly with you Lord. I really had to get on with it. Time pressure, you understand. Anyway, I am just checking out that is OK.' Worse still, activity can become the way we block spending intimate time with Jesus because we find it too uncomfortable and fear what it might involve if we truly listened to God first. And by lots of doing we can avoid the scrutiny of others for some time.

And when we catch the necessity of being with God first, as the most important thing of all, then truly doing for God is a deeply frustrating business because we are no longer able to rush ahead without spending a great deal of time being for God first.

What does Jesus want from us? What does Jesus want from our church? What does he want us to make progress in?

I think it is very instructive to examine the five intimate encounters that Scripture provides us with after Jesus' resurrection when he appears to five key figures in the gospel story. In each case Jesus seems to go right to the heart of their particular need and addresses it, and none of these examples begins with telling them to do anything. They all begin with their deepest emotions on their insides, in their very being.

Firstly, Mary Magdalene.

5 "Woman," Jesus said to her, "why are you crying? Who is it that you're seeking?"
Supposing he was the gardener, she replied, "Sir, if you've carried him away, tell me where you've put him, and I will take him away."
16 Jesus said to her, "Mary." John 20:15-16 (CSB).

Mary is weeping. She is missing Jesus. Indeed, she seems to have lost him for ever. Jesus, unrecognised by her, approaches and gives, her the thing she needs most of all: the comfort of his presence. She rushes into his arms. Of course, she has lost some of him - the opportunity to be enveloped by his physical arms has come to an end. This is a being thing, not a doing thing. The comfort of the presence of Jesus. And if we do not give Jesus the appropriate time and space in our lives, he will seem distant and we will lose him and that most precious thing of all. We need to give time to this. We need to stop the doing to regain it. Having satisfied her deepest need, then and only then, does he give Mary something to do. 'Go to the brothers and tell them.' A mere woman, as held by the society of the day, is called to be the very first evangelist. And none of this I guess would have happened if she had not first sought out the comfort of Jesus.

As we have seen when we read of individuals in Scripture, we are allowed to apply the teaching we gain to our insights of the individual bodies of local churches, to our CWASCs. Such CWASCs can seek out Jesus and find the comfort he gives. This principle remains true for the rest.

Then there are the two men on the road to Emmaus. Jesus meets them on the road. Cleopas and his friend are sad and puzzled. They also have lost the resilience to carry on. They certainly did believe something we are told, but their intellectual curiosity remains unsatisfied. Jesus once again remains unrecognised. They do not need a hug. It is all to do with their brains, their understanding, their comprehension inside the being of their heads. And once again Jesus satisfies this deepest need of theirs. He goes through the whole Scripture and shows them how it all makes sense. How what happened, had to happen. It was inevitable. And I can imagine these two men reflecting later, 'Yes of course. Oh, it is so clear now.' This story is different from the one in which Mary figures as Jesus does not tell them to do something as a consequence. He shows them something. He shows them how he may be recognised in the breaking of the bread. Then they do something at their own cognizance: it is to report back to the other disciples how it was in the breaking of the bread they recognised him, not through the intellectual understanding of Salvation History in the Scriptures. The full import of the significance of the holy communion and its place in the life of church is too much for me to unpack at this moment, but it is clearly significant and we need to give it some deep thought, especially as it applies to its practice in CWASCs. What is clear is that once again they start with the being before the doing.

Then we come to Thomas.

26 **A week later his disciples were indoors again, and Thomas was with them. Even though the doors were locked, Jesus came and stood among them and said, "Peace be with you."**
27 **Then he said to Thomas, "Put your finger here and look at my hands. Reach out your hand and put it into my side. Do not be faithless, but believe."**
28 **Thomas responded to him, "My Lord and my God!"**
John 20:26-28 (CSB).

Thomas is struggling inside himself, in his being, with believing. He has clearly some intellectual understanding, a bit like the two men on the road to Emmaus, but this is of a different order. He needs some concrete proof to crystallise his faith into something deep and meaningful. He is not being awkward or difficult. It is just that hearing what the other disciples say is not enough. It does not scratch the deep itch within him. My heart goes out to him. I find a bit of Thomas in me as I struggled at university to find Jesus. And Jesus is so kind. He comes to find him and gives him what he needs, as he did with Mary and the two disciples. And Thomas receiving what he needs breaks down.

Fourthly Peter. Peter's problem was betrayal. He had denied Jesus in the most spectacular way. Surely there was no way back from this? This is a very powerful one when we apply it to the CWASC. How does a CWASC betray God?

Jesus asked Simon Peter, "Simon, son of John, do you love me more than these?"
"Yes, Lord," he said to him, "you know that I love you."
"Feed my lambs," he told him. John 21:15-19 (CSB).

Oh yes there is a way back, but this encounter is far from cuddly/cosy like the previous ones. What Peter needs in his deepest being is to be given a second chance and an opportunity to repeat three times that the betrayal will not happen again. Have you had those moments? There is nothing you can do, no penance you can make by being cruel to yourselves or losing yourselves in endless Christian service to put this one right. It must be sorted in an intimate tete-a-tete with Jesus and it may involve many tears. And the structure of this passage is very interesting because on first sight it appears to undermine everything I have been saying and the point I am trying to make. For we read Jesus asking, 'Do you love me then go and do. If you love me go and do. If you love me, go and do. But notice right at the end, in case Peter has got the wrong end of the stick, and thinks he can put it right by doing, or we feel we can take it as justification for rejecting intimacy with Jesus in favour of activity. Jesus says to Peter and to us, 'Follow me.' An action of being and not doing.

Finally, Saul. He has been an absolute ******* to the Christian church. He has persecuted them, hunted them down, imprisoned them and killed them. Is there any way back from that? Of course, saying it like that we may find it hard to identify with Saul, but if I were to ask you whether you ever feel hatred, I am sure you would say yes, and if I probed you to discover the object of that hatred, I am sure at times you would say it was towards other individual Christians. Well not hatred, we might add, but I was jealous you might qualify. Case proven.

"Saul, Saul, why are you persecuting me?"
5 "Who are you, Lord?" Saul said.
"I am Jesus, the one you are persecuting," he replied. 6
"But get up and go into the city, and you will be told what you must do."
10 There was a disciple in Damascus named Ananias, and the Lord said to him in a vision, "Ananias."
"Here I am, Lord," he replied.
17 Ananias went and entered the house. He placed his hands on him and said, "Brother Saul, the Lord Jesus, who appeared to you on the road you were traveling, has sent me so that you may regain your sight and be filled with the Holy Spirit." Acts 9:4,5,10,17 (CSB).

Jesus identifies himself and immediately tells Saul to do something. He is to go and seek help. He is to surrender to other Christians. Jesus does not give him a ministry. That comes a lot later after much preparation. He is told to submit to the very Christians he is persecuting. It might have gone badly. It did not. Saul is so mortified by his behaviour and how wrong he has been that he stops eating and drinking for three days. The maximum time possible to be deprived of water before dying. What terrible thoughts were going through his mind? And if he was in any way human it would be remorse and self-pity that he had been caught out in such wrong doing.

In these personal meetings with Jesus, he calls them and us to first and foremost take time with him - and time we must give him.

Jesus craves to meet us in our deepest being. He offers us comfort when we miss him, he offers us intellectual understanding and wisdom when we lack them as we study his word. He offers to reveal himself in the breaking of the bread. He forgives us our betrayal and still finds us lovable and useful. And even when our personalities collapse and we are filled with deep hatred based, as it was with Saul, on a complete misunderstanding of Christianity, he redeems us and is willing to spend time with us. So also, these promises of intimate fellowship with Jesus are open to our church body.

In fact, we can find one further person who had an encounter with Jesus in these passages - a complete contrast. Of course, there is Saul - the one who does and does and gets it all wrong because he does not start with the person of Jesus. We nearly miss Ananias. At the very moment Saul is being humbled we find Ananias in prayer feeding his soul, being faithful to Jesus and giving time for them to open their hearts to each other. A wonderful example of action, of indeed the miraculous action of doing, proceeding from somebody who typifies what I am hoping we can now see. Here is Ananias who, after spending time with Jesus, remains nervous about doing the thing asked – to go and pray for Saul. He has heard bad reports about him. Yet nevertheless in the strength of God he goes and out and does what he had been commanded.

Am I against doing and serving? Not at all. Perhaps this will help.

My wife has taken up learning to play the piano. Watching her has left me astounded by how much time she spends alone with the piano practising to get it right. Concert pianists spend regular hours each day in an intimacy of understanding with the music they are about to play. Finally, only too aware of their inadequacies they go and play their hearts out.

May our churches give such quality time to Jesus and then go and play their hearts out for him. Amen.

In the end the simplicity of being speaks louder than activity.

SECTION D – IT CAN ONLY BE LOVE.

CHAPTER 26 – The Minister As An Example [Sample] Sent By God.

[17] I know, my God, that you test the heart and that you are pleased with what is right. I have willingly given all these things with an upright heart, and now I have seen your people who are present here giving joyfully and willingly to you. 1 Chronicles 29:17 (CSB).

[15] I will give you shepherds who are loyal to me, and they will shepherd you with knowledge and skill. Jeremiah 3:15 (CSB).

When I became the incumbent of my last parish 29 years ago the selection process was very convoluted and entirely dissimilar to the system of interview panels that are in place today. I felt courted and valued in a way that I am not sure that modern candidates do. The discovery of the parish vacancy was quite ordinary in that I scoured adverts in the Church Times and went to see the National Clergy Advisor. I even spent a few hours in 10, Downing street talking about a Queen's Appointment. My wife and I had hoped and therefore expected – a wrong premise I admit - to be called back to family connections elsewhere in the country. However, when I was asked to view a parish in East Anglia, I went to have a practice. Another worldly black mark against me!

However, I discovered that the parish and the archdeacon had a genuine desire to discover if I was the right person, indeed, if I was called by God to go there. The parish had to decide, so did the archdeacon, but most importantly I did too. To be frank it was not what I wanted, yet I could not shake off the feeling that they wanted me; and the archdeacon was very positive about it. I vacillated and sweated about it. The archdeacon told me that I would not really know until I said yes. I am still pondering that advice all these years later! Nevertheless in all this, and there was no sense that I had to sell myself which is the most telling difference from the custom today. In the end, I felt enough assurance from God that I accepted the call. I was there for 26 years. Every year my wife and I checked out with God as to whether we should remain and the answer remained yes. In fact, during some very difficult times, it was this continuing assurance that God had very definitely called me there, and wanted me to remain, that kept us warm at night.

Most of you who have had a similar experience will know that any call is a burden. At your darkest moment you will wonder if you are a bad priest, or a bad incumbent, in the same way that Saul was a bad king; and worse, at those times you see yourselves as this failure, perhaps so does God.

Saul was angry and unrepentant and, as far as I can see, I was not. Many of the great leaders we read of in the Bible were full of doubts. Moses felt quite unworthy and inadequate in the face of his call to extricate the Hebrews from Egypt. He pleaded to be excused because of his weak voice and fear of public speaking; Aaron was dragooned in to help. Gideon wanted the reassurance of a repeated miracle to get his mojo going. Jacob wrestled with God. There is no complete solution to such internal doubts. In any case they are the best way to keep you humble.

Another burden is to think that God has called you to be an example to your congregation. They certainly want to treat you as such. They expect a certain excellence as they live their Christian lives through you vicariously. Once, in all the turmoil of going back to first principles with God, when I acknowledged afresh the scale of some of the problems and the resistance I was encountering, I spent a fruitful time considering the difference between example and sample. The problem with being an example is you feel you should be a shining example. This is an alternative phrase for burnout. It can't be done. A sample, by contrast, is more like the miniscule offcut you get sent through the post when you are trying to match a piece of wallpaper, paint or material. It represents a possibility. I decided I could be a sample of what it was to be a Christian and it was OK if I was not a very good one. My people did not have to emulate me, which would be a burden to them, but draw close to an approximation, finding their own colour and texture of what it was to be a Christian based on the small sample I gave them.

One thing your congregation does need to have in you is confidence. There are various ways of creating this. You will have to find your own way, but I will give you one example, or is it sample? My church contained a lot of men of my father's age. My relationship with them did not go well at first. Then, in a flash of inspiration, I recalled that most of them had been in the forces during the war and would have come across a Padre, an officer. In a rather conscious effort, I styled myself on this familiar, yet enigmatic figure, and channelled being an officer with a dog collar on. With a degree of made-up authority and bonhomie I passed muster. It worked. Things improved immediately. I called them 'Sir' on occasion in respect of their age, but was firm and direct at others – like giving orders to NCOs.

The confidence you are trying to build is that they believe you know what you are doing, that if something fails you will get up again, dust yourself down and restart; that you are a person of reflection and prayer and that you take appropriately the authority that being a priest in the Church of England gives you. It is so important that you do not feel unworthy or ashamed. We need to take confidence from the very detailed selection process we underwent and, particularly, that our ordination did bestow on us a mantle of leadership and authority.

It is good to keep reminding yourself you are not alone, even when you want to be. There is a temptation to be paranoid and to hide behind your parish boundaries in fear that some other church is trying to poach some of your key workers.

You need to recall that the charge to the parish is shared with your bishop. This does seem a bit of an embarrassment, but why should it?

Can you image a parish priest ringing up his bishop and saying to the bishop, 'OUR parish is in a mess what are you doing about it? This is your responsibility as much as mine, you promised.'

A few raised eyebrows. But why? Is not this what it means to have joint charge?

Of course, there is not a blue print to build a parish priest. I still reflect on how unlike all my fellow clergy were in all the different chapters I attended. Surely, at times, we all must look as mad as a bag of frogs to each other. It is a wonder that such an eclectic eccentric group of individuals could manage to find any common ground. Yet we did!

I am and always have been Robin Pritchard, priest. All that I brought in my uniqueness of my character of gifts was sufficient for God to endorse and call me his priest. A cursory look at the Scriptures, studying one by one the lives of the judges, the kings, the prophets and the priests will confirm this. The Scripture is so wonderfully visceral about failure and weakness in leadership; in the leadership of the sinful men and women God called to carry out imperfectly his will. There is no homogeneity in priesthood and even the OT and NT differences in leadership and all its subtleties are found in the glorious multiplicity of joyful renditions of what it means to be a priest in the CofE.

The relationship between priest and his congregation is not entirely a friendship, although it can have those elements, or a marriage, although the vows resonates on similar frequency, or between siblings, or parents and children. The collar becomes like the ring of a nun, an illustration of a marriage with God in a common task. The metaphors are good, but so are the differences from them.

I must admit to some disquiet with those clergy who have eschewed the dog collar. This may be my age, but it is more my experience. While it lasts the dog collar is a wonderful key of entry. In my parish ministry I could turn up at a stranger's door step, knock and get invited in simply on the strength of the history and familiarity of me dressed as clergyperson. Let us not throw that away.

And it is so good that a fuss is made of the beginning of ministry in a church, with all its formal shenanigans. Induction and Institution feel so right and so empowering when you go through them. They are confidence building.

There is so much to enjoy, embrace and rejoice over being a priest in the Church of England.

CHAPTER 27 – Ministers' Dreams.

[23] The LORD answered Moses, "Is the LORD's arm weak? Now you will see whether or not what I have promised will happen to you." Numbers 11:23 (CSB).

As Christian ministers I think we long for miracles of ministry. By this I do not mean healings or financial gifts, although these are most welcome, I am thinking mainly of quick and easy solutions. Ministry is a long, faithful, hard and wearing slog – at the best of times. At the worst we see years of work unravel in a moment. This is not always because people we rely on to do something die. Others, often rancorously, throw in the towel and decamp to, as they perceive it, a 'livelier' church, just when you wish you could too. These disappointments are a bitter blow. A minister's dreams are often deflated. It is so easy to feel dissatisfied with the unhurried pace of change in your congregation, especially if it is a CWASC, because inevitably things in such churches happen much more slowly. Then there are the indescribable feelings resulting from a neighbouring CWALC pushing to open a church plant in your parish, when inside you are screaming, 'Why do not they send such a group of committed Christians to us? It could revitalise what I am doing. They mustn't trust me with their precious Christian pioneers!'

As a minister you are predictably judged by your results. Inevitably, the uninformed and unsubtle, often from a distance, will judge a minister by his church as we do a father by his children. If the outcome of your ministry appears to be the CWASC in which you minister, then that represents the value of what you are doing.

Truthfully, you should no more blame the industrious farmer for the crop he produces from a field of poor soil, covered in tree roots and rocks, that floods frequently, than to praise a lazy farmer who produces admirable crops from his rich-soiled, well-drained and sunlight-soaked field. It is so galling that worldly judgments are given so glibly in these situations. I cannot be alone as a young minister, probably unrealistically, to begin my work enthusiastically, full of a desire for adventure and fulfilment, to be cast down by such comments or the self-accusing thoughts that follow.

Much of a minister's work goes on inside his own head. I regularly went on self-led, quiet days, sitting in my car, overlooking the sea where, with my commonplace book and pen, I prayed and explored once again what I was doing. I accumulated several books over the years of such prayerful angst. At 69 and retired I have now shredded them! At the time they kept me sane.

We as ministers are works of God. I wait in hope that at the great judgment I will not be judged on whether I succeeded, but what I did and my faithfulness in it. In my early years of ministry, as I have already mentioned, I was taken in by the 'How I brought my church alive' books by famous ministers and tried to engage with and emulate some of their ideas. In the end I saw there was no blue print. I was on my own [except with the bishop!] and I was facing a unique situation with a unique personality and set of gifts. God had thrown me and my congregation into a great mixer and was blending us together - or more like a jewel grinder, to rub the corners off each of us.

Then there were the dreams. After finishing my formal education, I used to have exam dreams. I understand these are common. There were moments of panic in the night where I was trying to run away in the treacle of my thoughts and escape from situations where I turned up at an exam only to find I had revised the wrong thing, or my mind had gone blank, or my hand would not write.

After five years of teaching in a comprehensive I began to have teaching dreams – nightmares: being in the staff room and not being able to understand the timetable; wandering through deserted corridors to find my class; sometimes finding empty classrooms and other times facing strange, unrecognisable groups; finally to face deteriorating lessons as classroom control slowly eluded me and a riot developed, all the time fearing the headmaster would come and look through the glass panel on the classroom door.

Of course, now, I get ministering nightmares: wandering around deserted cathedrals looking for a verger, the bread and wine and a congregation; forgetting my sermon notes. So, it goes on. Yes, I have a troubled mind and my years of ministry have left a mark. My dreams reveal a deep level of anxiety about it all. Sadly, I have never had the reverse sort of dreams - where I find my church so full that the churchwardens are turning people away. Dang!

However, the greatest problem seems to be getting God to show as much interest in the situation as I feel. He seems to channel this careless attitude that is unattractive. I find him often so little concerned and with an obscure agenda that he does not share. He can be inscrutable. And bitterly for me, he does not seem to be one hundred percent behind my own agenda for growth and evangelism. 'What does God WANT? What DOES GOD feel?' I shout.

Just look for a moment at God's relationship with the Hebrews. He waits for years, centuries even, just to teach them a lesson. Nothing happens very fast. A generation or two passes before he says a bit more. In our desperation for church growth, we have become myopic about God's view on time and history. Of course, God will bring it all to an end when every stalk of wheat is gathered into his barn, but it does not have be done this week. He has a loose agenda about it. It is almost as though he gets distracted on his way there and sits down whilst we, his ministers, fume at the slow progress.

'Wake up wake up!' somebody is telling me. It is Jesus. I remember - I camped out last night with him. 'A bad dream?' he asks.

I nod mutely. 'The worst,' I eventually get out. 'I dreamt of success and then I dreamt of disaster. Which is correct?'

He puts some more sticks on the fire, then looks me full in the face and smiles benignly.

'Do you remember that bit in Numbers when Moses is having a hard time? The Hebrews were in the Wilderness and there was trouble about food.'

I indicate assent.

'Moses was worn-out. Remember what happened... we told him to bring seventy elders to the Tent of

Meeting and we would anoint them and take some of the spirit off him and put it on them, so they might help to bear the burden of the people and not have to bear it on his own.' [THIS IS BEST PRACTICE]

'Yes, I recall,' I said.

Jesus laughed 'Moses was not too pleased. He did not believe us. "I have got at least 600,000 soldiers and all the rest of the people, how on earth will you give us meat," he complained. And what do we say to him?'

I shrugged, the details were not in my memory, although as soon as I read it, I would remember.

'[23] **The LORD answered Moses, "Is the LORD's arm weak? Now you will see whether or not what I have promised will happen to you."** Numbers 11:23 (CSB).'

I nodded slowly and, after cogitating for a while, opened my mouth to say, 'But...'

He beat me to it, 'But you say...'

'And that is relevant to me because?' I was being a bit pedantic, but I knew that Jesus loved me and he would not take offence.

'Its relevance is in the words, in the metaphor, and in what you will make of it for your own situation.'

'You're at going to give me 70 elders?' I asked tartly.

He laughed aloud.

However, I was on a roll. 'You're going to give some of my spirit to other people? I am struggling with the little I have and you are going to take it back and weaken me. You're going to give us quail to eat?

His hand was fluttering, as much as to say, Shush. 'The thing is Robin; this is a dream too.'

I blew a raspberry. And then I woke up and I was on my own.

These dreams of success, nightmares of failure and Jesus as spirit invading my subconscious thoughts, feeding me with his word, speaking his words that are never as clear or as direct as I would wish, yet nevertheless containing some kernel of truth that raises my spirits. Moses struggled like I do: God intervened and he was helped, until next time. So, by fits and starts my ministry continues. Even on such basic fare my heart is fed and I can survive a bit longer.

In some strange way I find I stand with Abraham, Noah, Moses and a whole genealogy of people before me, looking back as the Mexican Wave of an intimate knowledge of God moves towards me down the centuries, as each in turn raises their arms to praise God. Then it is my turn and I lift my arms too, impelling it forward to my neighbour, on and on into the future. I picture my name on a long list of the incumbents of my church starting in 1301. I am a part of this picture, one thread, one part of some comforting metaphor. Praise God, my time has not been wasted and will not be.

CHAPTER 28 – Ministry In A CWASC.

[29] **And he named him Noah, saying, "This one will bring us relief from the agonizing labor of our hands, caused by the ground the LORD has cursed."** Gen 5:29 (CSB).

[2] **When the leaders lead in Israel, when the people volunteer, blessed be the LORD.** Judges 5:2 (CSB).

[3] **Joanna the wife of Chuza, Herod's steward; Susanna; and many others who were supporting them from their possessions.** Luke 8:3 (CSB).

My metaphor of being able to compare different church situations to different fields and soil types and geography has already been stated. And the solution would be to say that ministers ought to be proud to be called to ordinary situations - it is a privilege. Everybody swallows hard at that. For unless you feel a particular call to serve in a CWASC, it can feel like a death sentence to be sent into such ministry by chance.

When I began at my last incumbency my church was of fair to middling size, but it soon became apparent, as the years went by, and as society became indifferent to Christianity that a good number of my congregation's connection to church was through its structure and not through a genuine, lived-out faith. The National Church began to lose traction, on a Sunday for example. Sunday trading and social events beyond the church proliferated, children and parents were drawn away by Sunday sport. Uniform organisations, who in the past had regularly brought children to church, began to struggle to find committed leadership. I had to shut down my own Boys Brigade, to some dismay, not because they were no boys to join it, or even that there was a lack of offers to help from parents, but because there were no volunteers to be the committed officers, without which the troop could not run. Such deterioration of duty affected all corners of church life. My success, or failure as some would see it, in providing a mixed economy that included modern styles of worship disenfranchised those who felt it went too far from those who did not think I had gone far enough. So, my church, by degrees over many years - I was there for 26 years - became a CWASC. I know there will be some who immediately think I stayed too long and I can offer reasons why I did, but not excuses.

The received wisdom when I began my ordained ministry, at the age of 31, was that it was better to have priests with some experience of life, who had had a job in the real world. That philosophy seems to have disappeared. Similarly, it was thought best if incumbents moved on after a few years. Those in the game a long time will have seen a good many of these theories. I used to ponder this particular one, as I sat on a number of occasions in the Chancel of a strange church during an Induction, reading the memorial plaques of former incumbents who had spent 60 years in that place. Statistical research has shown that older ministers have a lot to offer: there is not an inexhaustible supply of young ministers with families to meet the expressed desires of congregations; those about to retire take the most risks; that ministerial strengths and effect vary throughout the years a minister stays. My own parish was constantly in a state of flux, in its socio-geographical profile. I was one of the unchanging aspects of it, a guardian of its spiritual history with an overview to speak of important things.

Clearly there are caveats to this, yet if a minister has a sense God wants them to stay in post and the congregation do too, and even the parish accept them as a spiritual person to turn to, change for changes sake loses its power.

Unfortunately, a CWASC has a false narrative attached to it, as mentioned right at the beginning of this book: small equals failure, equals weak. I believe that some ministers, rich churches and the diocesan hierarchy have become too eager to collude with this false account.

Let us imagine a field says Jesus. Here is a good expanse of good soil, unfortunately, there is also a footpath that leads from one corner to the next and quite a footfall of people using it. It is useless to plant seed on the compacted earth for it soon gets trampled and the Ramblers Association are as keen as mustard for it to remain as part of the National Footpaths Scheme. Walkers with sticks strike out here and there to push back the farmers crop, as they would an invading army. In one corner of the field there is a small outcrop of boulders. The farmer has never dug down deep enough to see if they are all connected underground. He cannot get any of his large mechanical equipment in that corner, but has allowed the Heritage Scythers to plant and harvest it free, if he has the wheat at the end of the day. Next to it is a dip. Most of the year it is fine, especially if it is warm, but in the spring, it can become a persistent pool and so a waste of land. Finally, some enemy, the farmer thinks it could be a cousin of his mother's family – the swine - planted some Japanese Knotweed among the brambles in the corner. This has a government warning on it and every year he needs to refence it, losing more of his field each time.

Who is the sower when we take this as a spiritual metaphor? In the original, it was Jesus. For my purpose it will be the priests of the CofE, or indeed any Christian church. They come in boldly with their seed bag and then look with despair as they see it has been divided up by parish boundaries. Someone, words escape me, has put a boundary down each side of the path, effectively making it one long thin parish. Similarly, with the pool, the rocks and the knotweed. The largest area is the good soil. All the ministers look covetously at it. The parishes are shared out and one trusts that God knows best and sends the right person to each parish. Even those with the good soil are not free from covetousness and sometimes think, because they are farming the good soil successfully, that the person with the rocky ground could do better - not that they have ever farmed on rocky ground, nonetheless, they are sure some of their principles would work. They are universal, right? Without even consulting the poor farmer, with their worn shoes from walking across the harsh ground, they look covetously across the rooftops at the poor person's plot, quite forgetting Nathan's rebuke of David, and considers whether they should do some sewing of their own.

I wonder, though, what is good soil? The poor widow only put in a mite, but was praised far more than the rich donors by Jesus. In terms of value added from what you start with and where you end up, it might be that the minister of the CWASC achieves far more in percentage yield increase, than the farmer of the large field of good soil.

In any case, we are missing the point: God has made it clear that all the original field, without exception, is to be planted, harvested and gathered in, and, not until it is, will he return to hear his farmers give account. Why does God persist in sewing seed in such poor areas? Maybe he should cut his losses?

There must be experienced farmers out there who are used to working on their own, who labour away without any reward and poor results, yet are the best to get a high yield from such impoverished ground. We call ministers in new situations pioneers with some pride, because it is new, it is heroic, but do not accord the same credit to those who work older seams. This is highly specialist work and involves the stress of coping with nobody apparently changing from year to year save growing older. What does that do to ministers? Does God allow 'perseverance' to be the main crop?

11 **My days have slipped by; my plans have been ruined, even the things dear to my heart.** Job 17:11 (CSB).

15 **Why do you crush my people and grind the faces of the poor?"** Isaiah 3:15a (CSB).

Do you wait until the end, to future years, hoping that they will be better tractors and fertilisers for these poor situations, or do you just get stuck in? Did not Jesus imply that we should, 'Send out the workers, the fields are full and ripe for harvest? There is enough land for everybody. Anybody fancy the parish that is a footpath? Footfall is a description used for high streets. Fancy being a chaplain to a shopping centre or hospital where everybody, except the staff, changes day by day?

There is something very peculiar in the old-fashioned sense, very 'strong bread', strong tasting about a CWASC. A CWASC shows most strongly the composition of character in a church. There is nowhere to hide in one, or from each other – the difficult ones cannot be marginalised or ignored. All opinions, even the unpopular ones, are on show. Each loose, wrong or missing thread shows up in the garment of a CWASC. It is impossible to form a fellowship group of likeminded people to avoid the rest. House groups cannot be homogenous; they are by nature gritty, a mixture of all ages and opinions. A CWASC issues a stark challenge to any minister to love the brotherhood/sisterhood. There is no dilution, no patches of homogeneity; it is as it is; one singular body with all its thoughts. It is also a test of ministry and a showcase of a church because a CWASC, without resources, is open to all sorts of challenges. Such a church need to exhibit more trust in God and his actions on their behalf. They appear to be starter churches is perpetuity, but this is OK.

CHAPTER 29 – Loving A CWASC.

[28] "For this is what the Lord GOD says: I am going to hand you over to those you hate, to those you turned away from in disgust. Ezek 23:28 (CSB).

All churches, however big or rich their congregations let God down. And he hates it!

[14] The LORD roused the spirit of Zerubbabel son of Shealtiel, governor of Judah, the spirit of the high priest Joshua son of Jehozadak, and the spirit of all the remnant of the people. They began work on the house of the LORD of Armies, their God, Haggai 1:14 (CSB).

I have this fear that should my wife Carol die before me, I will forget what her face looks like. We have been married 46 years at the time of writing. Of course, I have lots of photos, but the fear remains that when I am apart from her and the pictures, I will not be able to conjure it up. Or that if she went missing and there were no photo, I would not be able to create a photofit to find her. It is an unreasonable fear, for her face is the most familiar of all faces to me, even more than my own. I am too close. We are married, one flesh, that is how it is supposed to be.

If you embed as a minister in a CWASC for a good period you will experience a few of the same feelings. There will be no ring involved though. At times it will feel like a ball and chain. Unfortunately, we only have one word in English – love – to conjure up a whole host of feelings. At times I experienced many negative feelings about the churches I served in and myself for being stupid enough to go to them. In this potent mix that I would describe as love for my CWASC, there is self-pity, a sense of abandonment by God, punishment by God even, jealousy, loneliness, as well as growing self-reliance and pride at surviving with God's help. The people were too close at times, yet even in this it was difficult to find friends. They could not distinguish between me as the minister, at times speaking with a minister's voice, and the friendship I craved. Being called to a CWASC is like hearing a gentle knock on the door during the night and when you open the door there appears to be nobody there. Then, as you glance down at the step, you find an abandoned child. You have no choice - you must pick it up and take it in. There may be better people to care for this foundling you think; yet your own certainty in your Christian calling to ministry means it is hard to let the child go, and with this calling, when compounded by the deep resonating voice of God who called you specifically, what can you do. Of course, you might not have the child long, the bishop might take it away, but the likelihood is that unless you make a 'complete balls up' nobody else wants it! This child is not the most beautiful child in the world. There is not some hidden locket in its basket that speaks of a royal heritage; it is only the faint glimmer of Christ's love that shines forth. It is a bit slow in its development and finds it difficult to grasp the simple things. The other children churches are a bit wary of it and call it names and pick on its small size. Vague disabilities hang over it that make you ask all sorts of questions about what exactly is a healthy church. And yet - see how quickly intimacy can develop. It is not a self-reliant child and lacks all sorts of basic confidences that will need time and love to repair. It lacks any real homogeneity in its constituent parts. It is all shapes and manners; mainly bad manners. The bad-tempered few cause havoc with their temper tantrums and have a disproportionate effect on it. It needs to be hugged and held and reassured a lot. Yes, it has value. Yes, Christ loves it. Yes, it has a work to do, a great work that belies its size. Yes, it is unique. God's blessing enabled it to come into being in the first place.

Of course, its parents might have been a legendary church figure with a hugely successful parish ministry and this child is more like Jonathan's son, Mephibosheth, that the nurse dropped.

Then as you look closer you begin to see little specks of gold. There are people in your church who have been there all their life, from Sunday school onwards, and have served the church in that place humbly. They have constantly rolled their sleeves up and never complained. They love the building; they love the place in which it is found. They have longings of heart for those who are their friends and neighbours to find Christ, though they kind of believe it will happen through some sort of osmosis, because that is the only explanation they have for their own coming to faith. They come regularly and persistently to all the services. They are not very good at giving money, quite apart from having only a state pension, there is an unshakable sense in them that the church is rich. Ask them to support a missionary endeavour, however, or build a toilet and it is like opening a bank account and finding somebody has already put cash in it.

Of course, there are things that can be done and these good souls fear confrontation, yet will support a minister if they face off the bullies and the damaged ones. The good ones will even cope with a very public temper tantrum from the despoilers if it results in a victory for common sense, peace and quiet. They are all very good at reading people. They know you are an officer, and a teacher, and a judge, and policeman, as well as a priest. They expect justice for themselves and everybody else; a justice that might include that cataclysmic ruckus of the minister saying to somebody, 'Do not speak to me like that again,' and, 'When you behave like that you are not welcome at services.' They have expectations of you as a minister and they would never challenge you, but you can tell by their faces when you disappoint them. You've seen that look on your parents' faces before now.

On the very first day of my ordained ministry, I was walking from my curate's house through an alleyway to church for a service wearing my brand-new, clerical shirt and collar and a young boy coming the other way chirped up, 'Good morning, Father.' I do not come from the tradition where priests are called father or mother, I am not opposed to it, it is just unfamiliar to me. Yet it felt good, if surprising. Years of ministry have shown me that at the end of the day what a lot of people want from me is fathering. Even people my parents' age need this, a basic, directed love to bring them hope and dignity in their problems, or as they approach death.

Deeper relationships forged over longer ministries are of benefit. I am not holding up myself as an example, as I said earlier, I was a sample, am a sample. When I went to my last parish, I was 38 and when retired I was 64. At my beginning quite a significant number of people were at the age I am now, 68. I watched them age from their sixties into their eighties and I journeyed with them. It was a revelation and I was enriched by it, and see the echoes now as I begin a similar journey. Here is the thing:

I was not simply there for them as their priest: they were there for me. I hoped to enrich their Christian spiritual lives and I now see increasingly clearly that they made me the person I am today. I would not be this retired priest with PTO, if I had not been there with them all those years. I was in the tumbling drum with them.

As a decided anorak, I still have all my sermons. Occasionally, towards the end of my ministry I used old ones from earlier. I found they did not sit too well. I wasn't that person anymore who preached that sermon and neither were they. When I began my PTO ministry in a neighbouring parish to my new home, despite the thought, 'I have a readymade supply of sermons to last me for ever,' God made it clear that I was to write new ones. I have obediently done so. There are not many leftovers stuck at the back of the freezer in God's ministry. I am an older and hopefully wiser chef now, and know how to use fresh materials better.

I ponder occasionally what would happen if I were transported back in time to 1991 as I am now with all my experience and what I would do better, quicker or even do at all. I am not going to share it, but it would be different. Certain things I did too quickly, but overall, I prevaricated, or was afraid to do more, and now I would move on more quickly. When we had our first baby, I was in awe of her and worried about her fragility. As those of you know who are parents, babies are tough and can cope with quite a bit of manhandling to see to their needs. A CWASC is quite a tough church - see how long it has survived so far with so few people and so little resources!

What one cannot tell so clearly about oneself is how much one's love for another person or a church is tainted by selfishness. I cannot hide from myself that my love for my wife was because I wanted her to love and need me back. This is OK. Surely God's love for us is not entirely unselfish - he wants us to love him back. In fact, he is quite strict about it: he wants us to choose to love him and for him not to need to force us.

We enter ministry with so many conflicting emotions. It is not wrong to want to succeed and neither is it wrong to want to share Jesus with people. If you are entering ministry and you are not ready for the love song of Solomon then stop and reconsider.

The true saint in my parish was a wonderful, loving woman. I have alluded to her before. She had a facial disfigurement that meant she was not conventionally and never would be pretty. She and her husband were not able to have children. They adopted a disabled child. Her work in church never reached any great heights, but she was a tireless and committed personal worker, walking hundreds of miles, keeping touch with the elderly ladies in the women's group, offering a willing hand whenever she could, being my eyes and ears as to who was sick. I confidently expect her to be much nearer to Christ in heaven than I can ever get.

Is God calling you to ministry in a CWASC? It is not a lesser ministry. I am going to say that twice – it is not a lesser ministry. In many ways it the greater. And yes, it will be hard, and you will regret it, and feel self-pitying that everything takes so long, and often goes backwards, and that you have all the household worries about plant and resources. Nevertheless, you will find satisfaction and quiet joy in serving. And if God does call you there, and you sense his presence, you will have the reassurance that you are where God wants you and find that contentment that comes even in the face of adversity.

God will judge you by what you do, not by what you achieve. You may rest easy at the end of such a ministry knowing that it was enough.

And the worship. Of course, it can be a slog without proper music or enough voices to sing, but when the testimony of those ancient stones in the fabric coincide with a real expectation of God's presence and he answers that prayer, there is nothing better. Then, to walk to the back of the church and wait in the porch and receive what for them is a peon of praise, 'Good service today, Rector,' makes it worthwhile. And as the years go by… you see things, special things, as the years pass: I introduced passing the peace in 1991 to the church – there was some resistance – ha-ha. Over 20 years later the last of them gave in, they stopped crouching down in the pew pretending to pray, and joined in. You should have seen me smile and rejoice. This was a real treasure, far too good to miss by leaving early and scuttling off to a different church!

CHAPTER 30 – Providing A Ministry For A CWASC.

[9] **"The final glory of this house will be greater than the first," says the LORD of Armies. "I will provide peace in this place"—this is the declaration of the LORD of Armies.** Haggai 2:9 (CSB).

'And though she be little, she is fierce.' A quote from Shakespeare's *A Midsummer Night's Dream.*

Why can't a CWASC… why can't they be left to be content to be themselves?

When my mother became so senile that my father could no longer look after her at home and she was put into a nursing home, it was clear that at first, that she misunderstood why she was there. She thought she was there to work and hence caused the staff some problems in that she wanted to be the one who took the drink's trolley around and serve the residents. They wanted her to sit quietly and receive their ministrations. I have been in enough nursing homes to see that for the very old, sitting quietly dreaming away the hot afternoons with sleep and reminiscence and quiet conversation with a neighbour are all that they want. What is the problem with a CWASC being left alone to get on at its own pace? Why must we keep prodding it with a stick?

Prodding the CWASC with a stick is a new thing. It came in during my own ministry and it was provoked by financial considerations. Then financial poverty became linked inexorably to numbers in the congregation. The old-fashioned way was for the CWASCs to be pre-retirement parishes for the poor, old, doddering clergy to while away a few years before they gave up. It was an accepted thing. I am not espousing that. The CWASC needs vigorous, godly, energetic ministry.

I do not claim to be a financial wizard, I have no idea how to solve the Church's financial problems, but I am quite sure beating up 'small churches' - there I have used the dreaded phrase - is not the solution. I bet that if the CofE was rolling in money the false distinction between CWASCs and CWALCs would disappear and everyone would look more benevolently at the CWASC. In recent years a more congregational view of church management has grown up giving supremacy to individual congregations. The sense of community between churches and the knowledge that we are all in this together has been eroded. We are prepared to give start up pioneer work money quite rightly to establish themselves without the need to be financially viable to begin with. However, what if we have put too much hope in pioneer ministry? Just asking! Perhaps looking to find results beyond what can be expected in these days of indifference to the church. Of coursed God can work and bring thousands to salvation; the allure of these 'final days' and great awakenings is powerful, but history shows these to be rare events that are solely at God's discretion rather than the inevitable consequence of a simple comprehension problem that using right words and publicity will solve.

Perchance God might be more interested in unity – big churches working with small ones and indeed different denominations, and that this visible unity, if we could achieve it, might be a more powerful aphrodisiac in bringing people to Christ than evangelism on its own.

Small, fragile and weak can be beautiful. I still have clear memories as a child of weaving my way through a large crowd to get to the front in a way impossible now because of my bulk. Smaller enterprises have distinct advantages.

If by now I have not convinced you that a CWASC is of value I am never going to.

So how might we create a ministry for them?

I think first we need to create an expectation among clergy that to be called to such a ministry is a wonderful opportunity and one to be longed for. As a casual observer, it seems that, pragmatically, curates are sent to a CWALC to be trained. Without a second curacy to balance it they then find themselves as an incumbent without the necessary skills for a CWASC and of course, by then, they all want a CWALC.

It is clear to me that ministers in CWASCs need specific training and support. Which brings us back to money. I really do understand the anguish about money in the hierarchy of the church. I am sure I would feel the same if I was on a Bishop's council. It is my opinion that the only way forward at present is to provide a CWASC with a properly trained and ordained minister for free; free to the church and free to the diocese, apart from the training. Where could we look for such a group of ministers?

They already exist. There are many tentmakers in the CofE priesthood. They have had several acronyms over the years, but are now settled to SSMs for the present. Here is a group of dedicated minsters who are willing to offer their leadership skills and vocation for nothing bar a few expenses. They certainly do not have as much time as a stipendiary clergyperson; they need to earn a living too. It is up to others to say how overlooked they feel within the present structures of the CofE with its traditional emphasis on stipendiary clergy.

If I may dream for a moment. To do this we do need to be specific about numbers unfortunately. We need to define the upper limit for a CWASC. Perhaps an ER of no more than 20\30? Imagine a call to train SSMs to specific ministry within CWASCs. For those who respond: first, this would give them a clear sense of being able to own a particular area of ministry, to be valued for their skills in it and the satisfaction that brings. They would have a theological and ministerial formation specific for such situations. It would be a huge encouragement for some SSMs to be called to be Vicars. Compared to how they are at present categorised, it might make them gulp at the audacity of it! The CWASC would be released from the burden of contributing to stipends. Stipendiary clergy could go to the CWALC with a clear conscience. Large benefices that struggle with one clergyperson per fifteen parish might find each one re-established with its own SSM vicar. If the church can devote itself to keeping its plant in good order, or replacing it with a more cost-effective solution, then expenses are kept to a minimum. They might even have some spare cash to give to supporting larger church congregations and supporting pioneer ministries within their purview or at a distance. We need to disabuse the CWASC from only wanting a stipendiary clergyperson with a young family. They need education too.

Of course, I am naïve and hopeful distracted by love, with a certain persistent faith, but then I would not have suited being a minister of a CWASC would I? Ha-ha.

So, what has the CWASC learned from all this? Hopefully that all the things that are good and positive from God are also true for a CWALC.

The Reunification of Israel

15 The word of the LORD came to me: 16 "Son of man,
take a single stick and write on it: Belonging to Judah
and the Israelites associated with him. Then take
another stick and write on it: Belonging to Joseph—the
stick of Ephraim—and all the house of Israel associated
with him. 17 Then join them together into a single stick
so that they become one in your hand. 18 When your
people ask you, 'Won't you explain to us what you mean
by these things?'— 19 tell them, 'This is what the Lord
GOD says: I am going to take the stick of Joseph, which is
in the hand of Ephraim, and the tribes of Israel
associated with him, and put them together with the
stick of Judah. I will make them into a single stick so that
they become one in my hand.'
20 "When the sticks you have written on are in your hand
and in full view of the people, 21 tell them, 'This is what
the Lord GOD says: I am going to take the Israelites out
of the nations where they have gone. I will gather them
from all around and bring them into their own land. 22 I
will make them one nation in the land, on the mountains
of Israel, and one king will rule over all of them. They
will no longer be two nations and will no longer be
divided into two kingdoms. 23 They will not defile
themselves anymore with their idols, their abhorrent
things, and all their transgressions. I will save them from
all their apostasies by which they sinned, and I will

cleanse them. Then they will be my people, and I will be
their God. 24 My servant David will be king over them,
and there will be one shepherd for all of them. They will
follow my ordinances, and keep my statutes and obey
them.
25 "'They will live in the land that I gave to my servant
Jacob, where your ancestors lived. They will live in it
forever with their children and grandchildren, and my
servant David will be their prince forever. 26 I will make a
covenant of peace with them; it will be a permanent
covenant with them. I will establish and multiply them
and will set my sanctuary among them forever. 27 My
dwelling place will be with them; I will be their God, and
they will be my people. 28 When my sanctuary is among
them forever, the nations will know that I, the LORD,
sanctify Israel.'"
Ezekiel 37:15-28 (CSB)

Printed in Great Britain
by Amazon

79065012R00119